Trotter Trivia
Part Deux

Stuart Ball

Published by KDP Direct

Cover images

Trotter Van (Copyright Goldfinger/Wikipedia Commons)

Suitcases (Ilia Bystrov)

First published 2020

ISBN-13: 9798562560926

This book is dedicated to the memory of the Only Fools & Horses family members who are no longer with us –

Lennard Pearce, Buster Merryfield, Roger Lloyd Pack, Kenneth Macdonald, Roy Heather, Ray Butt, Gareth Gwenlan and, of course, John Sullivan.

Thank you for the laughter.

(Image copyright: Richard Johnson UK)

Also available by Stuart Ball

Trotter Trivia: The Only Fools & Horses Quiz Book

The Great British Sitcom Quiz Book

80s Quiz Master

A Question of Carry On

Proper Telly

Contents

Introduction

Trotter Quiz

Sir David Jason (Image copyright: Featureflash Photo Agency/Shutterstock.com)

Introduction

Au revoir! It might have taken slightly longer to arrive than it took Uncle Albert to get to the end of one of his war stories but the sequel to *Trotter Trivia: The Only Fools and Horses Quiz Book* is finally here! Yes, eight years after the publication of the first book and just when you thought it was safe to go back down the market, the cushty *Trotter Trivia Part Deux* has come to a battered suitcase near you.

While it may not be as impactful as the dramatic novel *The Indictment* by Rodney Trotter or as thorough and in-depth as the thirty-seven volumes of *Famous Historical Characters* that Rodders keeps in his bedroom, *Trotter Trivia Part Deux* is packed full of teasing quiz questions, informative trivia pieces and a full episode guide to Britain's most popular and beloved television sitcom of all time. For ease of use and to lessen the chances of you coming across any quiz answer spoilers elsewhere in the book, the quiz section has been placed at the front, while the guides to each episode come later. The answers for each quiz are conveniently located on the page after the relevant question set. Cushty, eh? As with the original *Trotter Trivia*, there are some questions which will get even the most hardened of Only Fools fans thinking furiously. Casual viewers have also been catered for with plenty of easier questions too.

I hope you enjoy this new journey into Trottersville as much as I have enjoyed compiling it. As a long-time *Only Fools and Horses* fanatic, writing these books really is a labour of love.

Bonjour!

Stuart Ball

Pukka or Pony?

This is the Trotter equivalent of a 'True or False' round. Answer 'Pukka' if you think the statement is true or 'Pony' if you believe it to be false.

1. The famous *Only Fools and Horses* theme tune was sung by Nicholas Lyndhurst.

2. The original choice of actor to play the part of Del was Kenneth MacDonald.

3. *Citizen Smith*, the first sitcom written by John Sullivan, featured an episode entitled *Only Fools and Horses*.

4. The original working title for *Only Fools and Horses* was *Readies*.

5. TV personality Paul Ross appeared as himself in the 2001 special *If They Could See Us Now*.

6. Buster Merryfield originally auditioned for the part of Grandad in 1981 but was unsuccessful.

7. In real life Nicholas Lyndhurst is a qualified pilot.

8. The part of Danny Driscoll, one half of the infamous Driscoll brothers, was written with actor Anthony Hopkins in mind.

9. Before becoming an actor, Lennard Pearce was a bank manager.

10. Actress and model Liz Hurley auditioned for the part of Cassandra.

Answers

Pukka or Pony?

1. Pony – John Sullivan provided the vocals.

2. Pony

3. Pukka

4. Pukka

5. Pony – it was Paul's brother Jonathan Ross

6. Pony

7. Pukka

8. Pukka

9. Pony – Buster Merryfield was once a bank manager

10. Pukka

Trotter Trivia

Buster Merryfield worked as the manager of the Thames Ditton branch of NatWest before retiring at the age of 58 and gaining employment with a repertory company.

Only Fools and Anagrams

Can you unscramble the following anagrams to reveal the names of twelve Only Fools and Horses actors?

1. Void Sad Jan

2. Hi Calls John

3. Jeep Steak Season

4. Arable Burp

5. Need Less Hours

6. Freestyle Bird Rum

7. Leaden Prancer

8. No Such Ill Hydrants

9. Tanned Chalk Demon

10. Perky Dog Collar

11. Mr Bidet Banjo

12. A Primary Truck

Answers

Only Fools and Anagrams

1. David Jason

2. John Challis

3. Tessa Peake-Jones

4. Paul Barber

5. Sue Holderness

6. Buster Merryfield

7. Lennard Pearce

8. Nicholas Lyndhurst

9. Kenneth MacDonald

10. Roger Lloyd Pack

11. Jim Broadbent

12. Patrick Murray

Trotter Trivia

Roger Lloyd Pack was the son of actor Charles Lloyd Pack who appeared in many British films of the fifties and sixties. Roger's daughter Emily Lloyd made her on-screen debut as an actress in the critically acclaimed 1987 film *Wish You Were Here.*

Only Fools and Girlfriends

Over the years both Del and Rodney have had a number of girlfriends. For each of the following girls, can you remember which Trotter brother they first went out with? Simply answer Del or Rodney.

1. Janice

2. Heather

3. Debbie

4. Imogen

5. June

6. Irene

7. Pauline

8. Miranda

9. Victoria

10. Trudy

Answers

Only Fools and Girlfriends

1. Rodney

2. Del

3. Rodney

4. Rodney

5. Del

6. Rodney

7. Del

8. Del

9. Rodney

10. Del

Trotter Trivia

The character of June Snell, played by Diane Langton, is the only one of the girlfriends mentioned in this round to have appeared in more than one episode. June made her first appearance in *Happy Returns*, then accompanied Del to the opera in *A Royal Flush*.

Only Fools at School

Going back in time to when Del and friends were young lads.

1. Originally known as Dockside Secondary Modern, what did Del Boy's school eventually change its name to?

2. Who was the rather psychotic headmaster of Dockside Secondary Modern?

3. In which year did Del, Trigger and Boycie all leave school?

4. Who was the goalkeeper for the school football team?

5. What does Trigger believe to be the name of the Italian boy who played in the school football team?

6. What is Trigger's excuse for walking into a 'Mind Your Head' sign while at school?

7. Which future enemy of Del's sat next to him in class?

8. Which television prankster does Trigger believe may have organised the school reunion in the Nag's Head?

9. What age was Denzil when he first became a pupil at Dockside Secondary Modern – 11, 13 or 15?

10. Rodney left school the proud possessor of how many GCE qualifications?

Answers

Only Fools at School

1. Martin Luther King Comprehensive

2. 'Bend Over' Benson

3. 1962

4. Denzil

5. Camaraderie

6. He couldn't read

7. Slater

8. Jeremy Beadle

9. 13

10. Two

Trotter Trivia

In real life, David Jason attended Northfield Secondary Modern School and, just like Del Boy in *Only Fools and Horses*, he played for the school football team.

Trotter A-Z – A & B

The answers to the first five clues all begin with A, while the final five answers all begin with B.

1. A - Heavily pregnant German student who features in the episode *From Prussia with Love*.

2. A – The name of Trigger's grandad, whose ashes end up in the possession of Del and Rodney.

3. A – The name of the canary that pet shop owner Louis sells to Grandad for £45 in *Who's a Pretty Boy?*

4. A - These musical doorbells play thirty-six different national anthems.

5. A – In *Go West Young Man*, Del sells a Cortina convertible to a man from this country.

6. B – This kindly old lady owns the Sunny Sea guest house in Margate but unfortunately she has no vacancies left for the Trotters.

7. B - Del orders this fruity cocktail when meeting Jumbo Mills for drinks in The Nag's Head in *Who Wants to be a Millionaire?*

8. B – The chairman of the tenant's committee who resigns his position in *Homesick*, leaving Rodney in the chair.

9. B – Seen briefly in Ashes to Ashes, this man is the Captain of Peckham Bowling Club.

10. B – This unseen character is the wife of Terry and mother of Shirley, Shane and Shaun.

Answers

Trotter A-Z – A and B

1. Anna

2. Arthur

3. Arturo

4. Antha Chime

5. Australia

6. Mrs Baker

7. Banana Daquiri

8. Baz

9. Bill

10. Brenda

Trotter Trivia

Nick Stringer, who played the unlucky Australian motorist who bought the clapped-out Cortina from Del in *Go West Young Man*, is one of only a handful of actors to have played two different roles in *Only Fools and Horses*. Nick also played the part of Del's former business partner Jumbo Mills in *Who Wants to be a Millionaire?* – once again with an Australian accent.

Del's Cocktails

We all know Del Boy loves a good cocktail but can you remember which ones he has ordered in the show? Answer 'True' if you think the cocktail has featured in an episode or 'False' if you think it hasn't.

1. Caribbean Stallion

2. Peckham Colada

3. Baileys and Cherryade

4. Tizer and Tequila

5. Grand Marnier and Grapefruit

6. Tia Maria and Lucozade

7. Rum and Vimto

8. Malibu Reef

9. Campari and Diet Coke

10. Peach Daquiri

Answers

Del's Cocktails

1. True

2. False

3. True

4. False

5. True

6. True

7. False

8. True

9. True

10. True

Trotter Trivia

The Caribbean Stallion was the very first cocktail ordered by Del in the show. He drank this rather exotic sounding concoction in the second episode *Go West Young Man*.

Only Fools and Music

That's all you youngsters are interested in these days. Noise, noise, noise!

1. What is the name of the pop duo that Raquel was once a member of?

2. Del once believed that Raquel had been top of the bill at the Talk of the Town in London alongside which music legend?

3. Which member of the Bee Gees made a cameo appearance in *Miami Twice*?

4. Who is the lead singer of A Bunch of Wallies?

5. What is the title of the hit single by A Bunch of Wallies?

6. Who are the regular band at the Shamrock Club?

7. In the episode *Sleepless in Peckham*, a David Bowie tribute act performs at the Nag's Head. Can you remember his name?

8. *Slow Boat to China* is the special song of which Peckham couple?

9. Del inadvertently starts a riot in *Fatal Extraction* by singing which song very loudly in the early hours of the morning?

10. Which cockney duo sang *Margate*, the song which played over the closing credits of *The Jolly Boys' Outing*?

Answers

Only Fools and Music

1. Double Cream

2. Otis Redding

3. Barry Gibb

4. Mental Mickey Maguire

5. Boys Will Be Boys

6. The Dublin Bay Stormers

7. Ziggy Sawdust

8. Del and Raquel

9. One Voice

10. Chas and Dave

Trotter Trivia

Chas and Dave were originally going to perform the famous *Only Fools and Horses* theme tune. However, just before recording was due to take place, the duo scored a huge hit with *Ain't No Pleasing You*, putting them in huge demand elsewhere. Writer John Sullivan eventually took on the task of singing the theme himself.

Who Said That?

Can you guess which characters spoke the following lines?

1. Bet you've held a few balls in here, m'lady.

2. Girls, seen much of Cinderella since the wedding?

3. Just be aware then, eh? Just be aware...

4. Del, desperate men on the run don't pop home to borrow a tin-opener!

5. You want to be a bit more careful about your health son. In the last half hour you've done so much boot licking you could be going down with cherry blossom poisoning.

6. Boomerang Trotter! Always comes back!

7. I've just come back from evening school. I'm learning Aikido.

8. You think I'm bald, don't you?

9. I have heard rumours Mickey Mouse wears a Rodney Trotter wristwatch.

10. I can almost see my grandad now, sitting by the fire, one leg on the fender, other one in the corner.

Answers

Who Said That?

1. Del in *A Touch of Glass*

2. Del in *Wanted*

3. Boycie in *Watching the Girls Go By*

4. Rodney in *Wanted*

5. Grandad in *May the Force Be with You*

6. Albert in *Strained Relations*

7. Mickey Pearce in *Happy Returns*

8. Jumbo Mills in *Who Wants to Be a Millionaire?*

9. Boycie in *Video Nasty*

10. Trigger in *Ashes to Ashes*

Trotter Trivia

The honour of speaking the very first piece of dialogue in *Only Fools and Horses* history went to Lennard Pearce, with Grandad uttering the line "That Sidney Potter's a good actor, ain't he Rodney?"

Only Fools on Holiday

Even yuppies with a busy lifestyle have to take a break every now and then.

1. In the episode *It Never Rains*, Del, Rodney and Grandad go on holiday to which popular Spanish resort?

2. While Del and Rodney look after Duke the dog in *Sleeping Dogs Lie*, Boycie and Marlene go on holiday to which island in the Indian Ocean?

3. What is the title of Rodney's painting which Del enters into a competition to win a holiday in *The Unlucky Winner Is?*

4. What is the name of the brand of cornflakes which is running the competition mentioned in the previous question?

5. Boycie owns a holiday cottage located in which English county?

6. To which seaside resort does the Jolly Boys' Outing travel?

7. Which Peckham couple find themselves in Miami at the same time as Del and Rodney?

8. In Ashes to Ashes, Trigger says he is looking forward to a holiday of 'discos, nightclubs, golden beaches and blue skies'. Where is he going?

9. In *Miami Twice*, Cassandra is unable to travel to Miami with Rodney as she is attending a work seminar in which English seaside resort?

10. After the Trotters become millionaires, Del books a holiday flying first class on Concorde to which Caribbean island?

Answers

Only Fools on Holiday

1. Benidorm

2. Seychelles

3. Marble Arch at Dawn

4. Mega Flakes

5. Cornwall

6. Margate

7. Boycie and Marlene

8. Ireland

9. Eastbourne

10. Barbados

Trotter Trivia

Each episode of the two-part *Miami Twice* featured a celebrity cameo. Richard Branson stood in front of Del and Rodney in the queue at the airport in part one, while Bee Gee Barry Gibb tended to his garden in Miami in the concluding episode.

Trotter A-Z – C and D

The answers to the first five clues all begin with C, while the final five answers all begin with D.

1. C – When Del once fooled Grandad into thinking he had won the pools, Grandad celebrated in the West End with this girl.

2. C – Name of the friendly female holiday rep in Majorca who believes Rodney is fourteen years old.

3. C – The surname of Eddie, a former East End publican who now owns the Mardi Gras in Margate.

4. C – The waiter at the Hilton Hotel, Park Lane who informs Del he has a telephone call waiting from his New York office.

5. C – In *Rodney Come Home*, Rodney has a business meeting booked with this representative of Classic Curtains.

6. D – According to the introduction given by Starlight Rooms' manager Eric, musical duo Raquel and Tony have just finished a sell-out season performing with Barry Manilow at this iconic Las Vegas venue.

7. D – The infamous Shamrock Club is located here.

8. D – The actor who played the Great Raymondo shares this surname with the sibling villains who turn up to wreak havoc in the episode *Little Problems*.

9. D – The name of Heather's young son who forms a bond with Del in *Diamonds are for Heather*.

10. The girlfriend of Albie Littlewood who had a fling with Del back in the sixties.

Answers

Trotter A-Z – C and D

1. Camilla

2. Carmen

3. Chambers

4. Charles

5. Mr Coleman

6. Desert Inn

7. Deptford

8. Driscoll

9. Darren

10. Deirdre

Trotter Trivia

The iconic Desert Inn, one of the very first resort hotels to open on the Las Vegas strip in 1950, was demolished in the year 2000. Frank Sinatra made his Las Vegas debut there in 1951 and, yes, Barry Manilow performed there for real too, although this was unfortunately without Raquel and Tony as the support act.

Only Fools and Barmaids

There have been a number of different faces behind the bar at the Nag's Head over the years.

1. Seen serving behind the bar of The Nag's Head in the very first episode *Big Brother* and then again in *The Second Time Around*, which barmaid did Del affectionately refer to as 'an old dog'?

2. In *Who's a Pretty Boy*, barmaid Karen complains to Del that the coat he sold to her dad has a hump in the back. What does Del give as an excuse for this?

3. Played by Nula Conwell, what is the name of the barmaid who retrieves a fiver from Del's pocket in *Watching the Girls Go By?*

4. In which long-running police drama series did Nula Conwell play the part of W.P.C. Viv Martella for nine years from 1984 to 1993?

5. What is the name of the red-headed barmaid seen pulling pints in the episodes *A Losing Streak*, *No Greater Love* and *It Never Rains?*

6 Which barmaid is working behind the bar of The Nag's Head in *To Hull and Back*?

7. In which feature-length Christmas special did Nervous Nerys first appear?

8. Which was the only other episode to feature Nervous Nerys?

9. Along with Mickey Pearce, who convinces Rodney that Nerys prefers men who are tough and macho?

10. What is Nerys' surname?

Answers

Only Fools and Barmaids

1. Joyce

2. The coat is made from genuine camel hair

3. Maureen

4. The Bill

5. Julie

6. Vicky

7. Dates

8. Sickness and Wealth

9. Jeavon

10. Sansom

Trotter Trivia

At the same time as playing Nag's Head barmaid Maureen in *Only Fools*, Nula Conwell was also starring in *The Bill*. She was scheduled to star as Maureen in the 1985 special *To Hull and Back* but due to her commitments in *The Bill* she was unable to appear.

Del's French Lingo

We all know that Del thinks his French lingo 'knocks 'em bandy' but which of the following phrases did he actually use? Answer 'Oui' if you think the phrase featured in the show or 'Non' if it didn't.

1. Bonnet de douche

2. Apres moi la deluge

3. Seulement des imbeciles

4. Chasse de forme

5. Boeuf Britannique

6. Envie d'un curry

7. Fabrique Belgique

8. Bain marie

9. Pichet mouche

10. Cocktail exotique

Answers

Del's French Lingo

1. Oui

2. Oui

3. Non (translates to 'Only Fools')

4. Oui

5. Non (translates to 'British Beef')

6. Non (translates to 'fancy a curry?')

7. Oui

8. Oui

9. Non (translates to 'fly pitcher')

10. Non (translates to 'exotic cocktail')

Trotter Trivia

One of the most popular of Del's French phrases amongst fans is 'bonnet de douche'. This rather exotic sounding phrase actually translates, rather simply, to 'shower cap'.

Only Fools in French

Can you identify these Only Fools and Horses episodes which have had their titles translated into French?

1. La Sortie des Joyeux Garcons (1989)

2. Cendres aux Cendres (1982)

3. Grand Frere (1981)

4. Une Touche de Verre (1982)

5. Yuppy D'amour (1989)

6. Heros et Mechants (1996)

7. Le Peril Jaune (1982)

8. Qui est un Joli Garcon? (1983)

9. The Pour Trois (1986)

10. Petards de Noel (1981)

Answers

Only Fools in French

1. The Jolly Boys' Outing
2. Ashes to Ashes
3. Big Brother
4. A Touch of Glass
5. Yuppy Love
6. Heroes and Villains
7. The Yellow Peril
8. Who's a Pretty Boy
9. Tea for Three
10. Christmas Crackers

Trotter Trivia

Yuppy Love, broadcast on January 8 1989, was the first episode to be broadcast with the longer fifty-minute broadcast time. This extra running time allowed writer John Sullivan to keep in more of the excellent material he was otherwise having to throw away due to the time constraints of a half-hour slot.

Only Fools in Pubs

You can't beat a good boozer can you?

1. After Mike is sent to prison for embezzling the brewery, who takes over the running of The Nag's Head?

2. What age was Trigger when he first started frequenting The Nag's Head?

3. Who was the winner of The Nag's Head talent contest which took place during the episode *Tea for Three*?

4. In *Dates,* Rodney mentions to Del that there is a stripper performing in which pub?

5. Harry Malcolm, who dies just before the annual publicans' ball in *Heroes and Villains*, was the landlord of which pub?

6. In which club do Del and Rodney first come across 'The Singing Dustman' Tony Angelino?

7. Who is the owner of the 121 Club, regularly frequented by Del in *Fatal Extraction*?

8. In which local casino does Del first make the acquaintance of supposed jewellery dealer Arnie?

9. Located in New Cross, which club do Del and Rodney visit on Christmas night in the episode *Christmas Crackers*?

10. In which episode does Mike take over as landlord of The Nag's Head?

Answers

Only Fools in Pubs

1. Sid

2. Sixteen

3. Albert

4. Coach and Horses

5. Crown and Anchor

6. Down by the Riverside

7. Ronnie Nelson

8. The One Eleven Club

9. Monte Carlo Club

10. Who's a Pretty Boy?

Trotter Trivia

The original script for *Heroes and Villains* saw the character of Harry Malcolm, on his deathbed, gaining revenge on Del for a past demeanour by sending him on a search for non-existent treasure.

Peckham Yellow Pages

The following clues all relate to businesses and establishments located in Peckham.

1. Tanya is the receptionist here.

2. Del is certain he is going to be the millionth customer at this supermarket.

3. Del books this venue as a rehearsal room for Raquel and Tony, so that they can get ready for their big night at The Starlight Rooms.

4. Trigger's grandad was a lifelong member at this local sporting venue.

5. Before changing its name, this business was known simply as Ron's Cash and Carry.

6. Mr Chin is the owner of this Chinese takeaway.

7. Del proposes to Heather in this Indian restaurant.

8. It may be more expensive in this convenience store but at least they smile when they take your money.

9. Del and Boycie strike a deal to supply the manager of this restaurant with fresh fish.

10. Before walking off into the sunset as millionaires, Del suggests to Rodney and Albert that they all go for a meal at this Chinese restaurant.

Answers

Peckham Yellow Pages

1. Peckham Exhaust Centre

2. Top Buy Superstore

3. Jesse Jackson Memorial Hall

4. Peckham Bowling Club

5. Advanced Electronics Research & Development Centre

6. The Golden Lotus

7. The Star of Bengal

8. Patel's Multimart

9. Mario's

10. The Golden Dragon

Trotter Trivia

In addition to Del speaking about Patel's Multimart in *The Longest Night*, the same convenience store is also mentioned a few years later in *The Unlucky Winner Is*. Nervous of his burgeoning relationship with Cassandra, Rodney is advised by Del that Patel's now has a selection of condoms situated by the phone card counter.

Only Fools and Relations

It's all in the family...

What relation is...

1. ...Reg to Del?

2. ...Grandad to Albert?

3. ...Renee Turpin to Trigger?

4. ...Albert to Del?

5. ...Marlene to Bronco?

6. ...Dora Lane to Marlene?

7. ...Lisa to Trigger?

8. ...Stan to Del?

9. ...Ruby to Slater?

10. ...Cassandra to Alan?

11. ...Tyler to Boycie?

12. ...Denzil to Carl?

13. ...Alice to Trigger?

14. ...Audrey to Raquel?

15. ...Damien to Rodney?

Answers

Only Fools and Relations

1. Father

2. Brother

3. Aunt

4. Great Uncle

5. Sister

6. Mother

7. Niece

8. Cousin

9. Mother

10. Daughter

11. Son

12. Brother

13. Grandmother

14. Mother

15. Nephew

Trotter Trivia

When Lennard Pearce died in December 1984, one of the original ideas was to bring an elderly female character into the show. However the plan was abandoned when John Sullivan realised it would be unseemly to have an elderly lady being regularly pushed in to the back of a three-wheel van!

Trotter A-Z – E and F

The answers to the first five clues all begin with E, while the final five answers all begin with F.

1. E – The name of the adult shop owned by Dirty Barry.

2. E – Del and Jumbo Mills once set up a seafood stall outside The Nag's Head trading under this name.

3. E – This policeman, who pulls up the Trotters for speeding in *The Russians are Coming*, is on the lookout for some stolen summer gear as he and his wife are planning a trip to Corfu.

4. E – The name of one of the fifty inflatable dolls which Del purchases from Denzil in *Danger UXD*.

5. E – This acquaintance of Del's, whom we meet at the Monte Carlo Club in *Christmas Crackers*, shares his name with Boycie's dog from *The Green Green Grass*.

6. F – The nickname which Rodney bestows upon Sid's café in *A Royal Flush*.

7. F – The surname of Bobby, former husband of Pauline Harris, who is now buried in the cemetery in Blackshaw Road.

8. F – Former occupation of Frederick Robdal when he served in the Navy.

9. F - The number of hours that the Trotters are held hostage in a supermarket in *The Longest Night*.

10. F - The surname of Tubby, former crewmate of Albert's, who died in Palermo Harbour after dropping a depth charge in nine feet of water.

Answers

Trotter A–Z – E and F

1. Ecstasy

2. Eels on Wheels

3. Eric

4. Erotic Estelle

5. Earl

6. Fatty Thumb

7. Finch

8. Frogman

9. Fourteen

10. Fox

Trotter Trivia

Character actor Derek Newark, who played policeman Eric in *The Russians are Coming*, also appeared in two other John Sullivan-penned series. He was a car salesman in a 1979 episode of *Citizen Smith* and played the character Eddie Brown in two episodes of *Just Good Friends* in 1984.

Only Fools and Animals

Taking a walk on the wild side.

1. Which of the Nag's Head regulars likes to keep tropical fish?

2. In the episode *Fatal Extraction*, what type of pet does Del buy Damien for Christmas?

3. What is the name of Denzil and Corrine's canary?

4. What breed of dog is Marlene's pride and joy Duke?

5. Thinking they were sleeping pills, who once swallowed Duke's vitamin pills by mistake?

6. What breed of dog do Boycie and Marlene have as a pet in *The Green Green Grass*?

7. What type of creature caused Rodney to fall off his skateboard while competing in a skateboard derby in Majorca?

8. What type of animal is missing from Del's big film idea – *There is a BLANK Loose in the City*?

9. Who does corgi Nero belong to?

10. What is the name of the racehorse owned by the Duke of Maylebury?

Answers

Only Fools and Animals

1. Boycie

2. Gerbil

3. Sylvester

4. Great Dane

5. Albert

6. Rottweiler

7. Lizard

8. Rhino

9. Janice

10. Handsome Sansom

Trotter Trivia

Earl the Rottweiler's kennel from *The Green Green Grass* still exists in the grounds of John Challis' house in rural Shropshire, as does farm manager Elgin Sparrowhawk's shed.

Only Fools and Anagrams 2

Can you unscramble the following anagrams to reveal the names of ten Only Fools and Horses characters?

1. Radar Spray Cans

2. Ray Ran Lap

3. Keep Racy Mice

4. Able Ceremony

5. Retort Battler

6. Sly Nordic Land

7. Mentor Ate Dirt

8. Yellow Stall

9. Pale Rap Army

10. Shuns Angry Boneheads

Answers

Only Fools and Anagrams 2

1. Cassandra Parry

2. Alan Parry

3. Mickey Pearce

4. Marlene Boyce

5. Albert Trotter

6. Danny Driscoll

7. Damien Trotter

8. Solly Atwell

9. Pamela Parry

10. Brendan O'Shaughnessy

Trotter Trivia

The character of Marlene, played by Sue Holderness, was originally planned to appear in just one episode but proved so popular with viewers she was brought back for more.

Middle Names

Can you guess which Peckham residents have the following middle names?

1. Charlton

2. Aubrey

3. Louise

4. Kitchener

5. Gladstone

6. Derek

7. Edward

8. Mavis

Answers

Middle Names

1. Rodney

2. Boycie

3. Cassandra

4. Grandad

5. Uncle Albert

6. Damien

7. Del

8, Joan Trotter

Trotter Trivia

Del's middle name of Edward was also the first name of Grandad, although this was never mentioned in any episodes of the show.

Who's Rachel?

The following quotes from the series all have the names of famous people missing from them. Can you fill in the blanks?

1. You know, it's only E-Type Jaguars and BLANK that make me feel proud to be British these days. (*Boycie*)

2. They get hold of this private detective you know, like a sort of BLANK type geezer to try and solve the crime. (*Del*)

3. The Boycie Video and Leisure Arts Company is proud to present the British premiere of *Night Nurse*, from the novel by BLANK. (*Boycie*)

4. Well, that's going to limit the conversation then, innit? I mean, they make BLANK look intelligent! (*Boycie*)

5. If it's a girl they're calling it BLANK after an actress and if it's a boy they're calling it Rodney, after Dave. (*Trigger*)

6. BLANK? More like Bathe It Daily! (*Del*)

7. I remember Lisa. Scruffy little mare weren't she? Had more candlesticks than BLANK. (*Rodney*)

8. She was a beautiful woman, a bit like Ginger Rogers. Last time I saw here she looked more like BLANK (*Albert*)

9. All you need is a couple of wizards and some little git with BLANK glasses and then we're off. (*Del*)

10. I'd rather play Dixon of Dock Green. I mean, he can't dribble like BLANK. (*Del*)

Answers

Who's Rachel?

1. Sebastian Coe

2. Charlton Heston

3. Enid Blyton

4. Grant Mitchell

5. Sigourney (Weaver)

6. David Bailey

7. Liberace

8. Fred Astaire

9. John Lennon

10. Jimmy Greaves

Trotter Trivia

Hollywood legend Charlton Heston was also mentioned in the 1989 episode *Little Problems,* as Del explained to Marlene that Rodney's middle name of Charlton came not from the film star but instead from his mum's liking for Charlton Athletic football club.

The Only Fools Soundtrack

The following songs have all featured on the soundtrack of various Only Fools and Horses episodes (titles in brackets). Can you name the artists for each one?

1. Merry Christmas Everybody (*Mother Nature's Son*)

2. Holding Back the Years (*Little Problems*)

3. Where is the Love? (*Little Problems*)

4. Zoom (*Diamonds are for Heather*)

5. Everybody's Talkin' (*The Jolly Boys' Outing*)

6. Burning Bridges (*Dates*)

7. The Mighty Quinn (*Class of 62*)

8. Uncle Albert (*He Ain't Heavy He's My Uncle*)

9. 2-4-6-8 Motorway (*The Jolly Boys' Outing*)

10. Lady in Red (*Yuppy Love*)

Answers

Only Fools and Music 2

1. Slade

2. Simply Red

3. Will Downing and Mica Paris

4. Fat Larry's Band

5. Nilsson

6. Status Quo

7. Manfred Mann

8. Paul McCartney

9. Tom Robinson

10. Chris De Burgh

Trotter Trivia

The end credits of *Animal Instincts*, a 2009 episode of *The Green Green Grass*, featured rock legends Status Quo performing the theme tune.

Only Fools and the Law

Taking a look at law and order in Peckham.

1. What is the name of the policewoman who Rodney takes out on a date in *Long Legs of the Law*?

2. Also in *Long Legs of the Law*, which record by The Police does Del say Rodney owns?

3. When Slater returns to Peckham in *To Hull and Back*, what is his rank in the police force?

4. What is the name of Slater's assistant?

5. Which member of the Jolly Boys' Outing was arrested for kicking a football at a police officer?

6. In which episode does Del mistakenly believe a female police officer to be a stripogram?

7. Which of the Nag's Head regulars live next door to a Chief Inspector?

8. Who claims to have never considered a career in the police force because he is ambitious?

9. In *The Russians are Coming*, what is the name of the unseen young police officer looking for his first arrest?

10. When the Trotters go on holiday to Spain in *It Never Rains*, Grandad is arrested for committing what offence?

Answers

Only Fools and the Law

1. Sandra

2. Walking on the Moon

3. Detective Chief Inspector

4. Hoskins

5. Rodney

6. Dates

7. Boycie and Marlene

8. Rodney

9. Wayne

10. Jaywalking

Trotter Trivia

The beach scenes in *It Never Rains* were filmed in the county of Dorset, with Studland Beach standing in for its Benidorm counterpart.

Trotter A-Z – G and H

The answers to the first five clues all begin with G, while the final five answers all begin with H.

1. G – The occupation of the character Tom Witton in *Friday the 14th*.

2. G - The first name of Grandad and Albert's brother, who fought at Passchendaele during World War I.

3. G - Rodney becomes an unwilling lifelong member of this group in *The Unlucky Winner Is*.

4. G – The surname of Lennox, otherwise known as 'The Shadow'.

5. G – Del was once a contestant on this television game show hosted by Jonathan Ross.

6. H – The coach driver who is overcome by fumes in *The Jolly Boys' Outing*.

7. H - Diamonds are for…

8. H – The first name of the fourteenth Duke of Maylebury, who is also second cousin to the Queen.

9. H - Albert met this girl in a bar near the docks in Hamburg just after the war and promptly fell in love with her.

10. H - While attending a banking conference in Guernsey, Cassandra stayed at this hotel.

Answers

Trotter A-Z – G and H

1. Gamekeeper
2. George
3. Groovy Gang
4. Gilbey
5. Gold Rush
6. Harry
7. Heather
8. Henry
9. Helga
10. Highcliff Hotel

Trotter Trivia

Gold Rush, the game show hosted by Jonathan Ross in *If They Could See Us Now*, was an obvious parody of the real-life quiz *Who Wants to Be a Millionaire?* Producers of *WWTBAM* were reluctant to allow the show to appear in *Only Fools and Horses*, leading to writer John Sullivan creating his own version on which Del could appear as a contestant.

Only Fools and Doctors

An apple a day keeps the doctor away, but look what happened to Snow White...

1. The Trotter family GP for many years, which doctor comes out to treat Grandad in *Homesick*?

2. When suffering with stomach pain in the episode *Sickness and Wealth*, Del visits the surgery hoping to see which doctor?

3. What is the name of the doctor who has now taken over the surgery?

4. When Del is hospitalised in the episode *Sickness and Wealth* with a mystery illness, what does Albert think may be wrong with him?

5. What does Del's mystery illness turn out to be?

6. In the episode *Chain Gang*, what are the names of Arnie's two sons, who disguise themselves as ambulance men as part of their father's con?

7. In *Chain Gang*, after Arnie fakes a heart attack in the middle of a restaurant, who pretends to be a doctor in order to retrieve the briefcase attached to Arnie's wrist?

8. Who worked for a short time at Newcastle Infirmary, before fleeing with 57 blankets, 133 pairs of rubber gloves and the chief gynaecologist's Lambretta?

9. According to Del, who trained as a chef at the ear, nose and throat hospital?

10. When Raquel is giving birth to Damien, Del gets excited when he thinks he can see the baby's head with a full head of hair. What is he actually looking at?

Answers

Only Fools and Doctors

1. Dr Becker

2. Dr Meadows

3. Dr Shaheed

4. Green parrot disease

5. Irritable bowel syndrome

6. Gary and Steven

7. Boycie

8. Reg Trotter

9. Grandad

10. The midwife's wig

Trotter Trivia

Although green parrot disease is a fictional ailment, it is possible for humans to catch a disease called psittacosis, also known as parrot fever. It is a respiratory infection which can be transmitted to humans from infected birds such as parrots, parakeets and budgerigars.

Guess the Year

This one is tough so I have made it a multi-choice round.

1. In *The Unlucky Winner Is*, Del alters the date of birth on Rodney's passport to this year.

A. 1964 B. 1974 C. 1984

2. Joan Trotter's best friend Renee Turpin moved from Peckham in this year.

A. 1963 B. 1965 C. 1969

3. The year that Del's best mate Albie Littlewood died after taking a shortcut across the railway line.

A. 1955 B. 1962 C. 1965

4. Del and Rodney's mum Joan died on the 12th of March this year.

A. 1964 B. 1966 C. 1968

5. In this year, Albert's ship docked in Hamburg and he met the nine-fingered Helga in a bar near the docks.

A. 1941 B. 1945 c. 1946

6. Freddie Robdal's gang successfully stole over a quarter of a million pounds in gold bullion in this year.

A. 1953 B. 1963 C. 1973

7. In this year, Auntie Rose told Grandad he could come down to visit her in Clacton at any time.

A. 1937 B. 1947 C. 1957

8. Grandad was deported from Spain and all her territories and dominions in this year.

A. 1936 B. 1939 C. 1949

Answers

Guess the Year

1. B 1974
2. B 1965
3. C 1965
4. A 1964
5. C 1946
6. B 1963
7. B 1947
8. A 1936

Trotter Trivia

The most revered date on the *Only Fools and Horses* calendar is September 8 1981, as this is the day that the very first episode, *Big Brother*, was broadcast to the nation on BBC1. Isn't it about time this date was made a national holiday? Only Fools Day has a nice ring to it, don't you think?

Only Fools and Anagrams 3

Can you unscramble the following anagrams to reveal the names of ten more Only Fools and Horses characters?

1. Red Otter Trek

2. Arty Loser

3. Quarrel Tuner

4. Ill Mum Jobs

5. Skim If Here

6. No Toy Leaning

7. Old Snot Lyric

8. Pedigree Trials

9. Mute Hear Agency

10. Entire Prune

Answers

Only Fools and Anagrams 3

1. Derek Trotter

2. Roy Slater

3. Raquel Turner

4. Jumbo Mills

5. Mike Fisher

6. Tony Angelino

7. Tony Driscoll

8. Elsie Partridge

9. Eugene Macarthy

10. Renee Turpin

Trotter Trivia

Jim Broadbent, who memorably portrayed despicable bent copper Roy Slater in three episodes, was one of the original favoured choices to play the part of Del Boy, along with comic actor Enn Reitel. After both turned the role down for varying reasons, *Open All Hours* star David Jason was given the opportunity and the rest is history.

Trotter A-Z – I and J

The answers to the first five clues all begin with I, while the final five answers all begin with J.

1. I - The Trotters sailed across to Holland in this boat.

2. I – In *To Hull and Back*, Rodney is worried that this girl is getting a bit serious, until he sees her with another man.

3. I – Albert's bad back is miraculously cured after just a few minutes treatment with this massager.

4. I – This bad-tempered woman works for Mrs Cresswell at the Villa Bella in Margate.

5. I – In *Cash and Curry*, Mr Ram claims to own a chain of restaurants that serve cuisine from this country.

6. J – In *The Frog's Legacy*, Rodney gets a job working for this local undertaker.

7. J – The name of the tutor at the computer science evening class attended by Rodney.

8. J – The young son of Del's old flame June Snell who lets down the tyres on Del's van.

9. J – The explosives expert who perished along with Freddy Robdal after an accident involving dynamite.

10. J – The wife of Stephen, Cassandra's boss at the bank.

Answers

Trotter A-Z – I and J

1. Inge
2. Imogen
3. Inframax Deep Penetration Massager
4. Inga
5. India
6. Mr Johan
7. Mr Jamille
8. Jason
9. Jelly Kelly
10. Joanne

Trotter Trivia

Mentioned in the 1987 Christmas special *The Frog's Legacy* and played by Paul Putner in the *Only Fools* prequel *Rock and Chips*, the real first name of Freddie Robdal's partner in crime Jelly Kelly is Gerald.

More 'Who Said That'?

Can you guess which characters spoke the following lines?

1. If Lord Krishna himself couldn't help us, I really don't think Esther Rantzen would stand much chance.

2. He's got 2 'O' Levels and he thinks he's Bamber Gascoigne's vest.

3. A doctor told Snow White to eat more fruit and look what happened to that poor cow.

4. Turn it up, Del Boy. Trigger couldn't organise a prayer in a mosque.

5. If he bites you, don't scream. He's highly strung.

6. What's an ovum?

7. What are the chances of you bumping into a bald-headed, anti-apartheid, deep-sea diving Bros fan who has a Betamax video recorder, likes Romanian Riesling and whose name is Gary?

8. This is all on the slate. I've got so many of his slates under here I could retile me bloody roof.

9. I've been chased by a gendarme, attacked by Pussycat Willum and almost caught rabies and it's all this dipstick's fault.

10. Little sod threw his breakfast all over me.

Answers

More 'Who Said That'?

1. Mr Ram in *Cash and Curry*

2. Del in *Cash and Curry*

3. Del in *Stage Fright*

4. Boycie in *Class of '62*

5. Marlene in *Sleeping Dogs Lie*

6. Albert in *Heroes and Villains*

7. Raquel in *Mother Nature's Son*

8. Mike in *Miami Twice (Part 1)*

9. Del in *Healthy Competition*

10. Albert in *Mother Nature's Son*

Trotter Trivia

In the same year that Renu Setna portrayed Mr Ram in the Only Fools episode *Cash and Curry*, the veteran character actor also appeared alongside David Jason in an episode of *Open All Hours* as a VAT inspector.

Only Fools and Marriage

Everyone loves a good wedding.

1. Who was Raquel's first husband?

2. How long was Raquel married to her first husband?

3. When Rodney and Cassandra get married, where do they hold the reception afterwards?

4. Where do Rodney and Cassandra spend their honeymoon?

5. What is the name of Uncle Albert's wife, whom he has compared to both Ginger Rogers and Fred Astaire?

6. When younger, Grandad had an extra-marital affair with Trigger's gran. What was her name?

7. At the wedding reception of Trigger's niece Lisa and fiancé Andy, who describes Andy's family as having 'big hats and no drawers'?

8. According to Marlene, what is depicted on the dinner service that she and Boycie have given to Lisa and Andy as a wedding gift?

9. According to Rodney, what is depicted on the dinner service that he and Del have given to Lisa and Andy as a wedding gift?

10. Which couple celebrate their twentieth wedding anniversary in the episode *Video Nasty*?

Answers

Only Fools and Marriage

1. Roy Slater

2. Four years

3. Upstairs room of The Nag's Head

4. Rimini

5. Ada

6. Alice

7. Aunt Renee

8. Changing seasons of the English countryside

9. Scenes from Tenko

10. Boycie and Marlene

Trotter Trivia

Appearing in nine episodes of the classic drama series *Tenko* in 1982, actress Josephine Welcome would go on to play the part of Dr Shaheed in the 1989 Only Fools episode *Sickness and Wealth*.

Trotter A-Z – K and L

The answers to the first five clues all begin with K, while the final five answers all begin with L.

1. K - Uncle Albert claims that his life was once saved during World War II by this naval captain's wig.

2. K – Rodney pretends he lives in this affluent street when Cassandra first offers to give him a lift home.

3. K – According to Uncle Albert, this man is a very bad dominoes player.

4. K – The daughter of Bronco Lane, who breaks her arm after climbing on to a chair to look at a plane.

5. K – The husband of Del's cousin Audrey, who, along with his wife, emigrated after sending Albert to Sainsbury's with a shopping list.

6. L – Boycie once spent time in prison after trying to bribe the mayor of this London borough.

7. L – This man is the owner and manager of the Shamrock Club.

8. L – Trigger's former colleague at the council depot, this girl's 'funny eye' meant Trigger never knew whether she was looking at him or seeing if the bus was coming.

9. L – Not long before Rodney was born, his mother became friendly with a musician from this club.

10. L - The surname of Italian pet shop owner Louis.

Answers

Trotter A-Z – K and L

1. Captain Kenworthy
2. King's Avenue
3. Knock Knock
4. Kylie
5. Kevin
6. Lambeth
7. Liam
8. Linda
9. Locarno
10. Lombardi

Trotter Trivia

Despite being born in Birmingham, actor Anthony Morton had a habit of playing Italian characters in John Sullivan sitcoms. In addition to his role in the Only Fools episode *Who's a Pretty Boy?* as pet shop owner Louis, Morton played an Italian police captain in the 1980 Christmas special of Sullivan's first sitcom *Citizen Smith*.

Around Peckham

The answers to the following clues are all places you might find on your sat nav while driving around Peckham.

1. The name of the tower block where the Trotter family live.

2. The tower block where Del's old flame June Snell resides.

3. Dirty Barry's 'personal' shop is located here.

4. Boycie and Marlene live at number 17 in this road.

5. Uncle Albert was born in this road.

6. The young Chinese boy who fixes Del's video recorders lives in this tower block.

7. When Grandad was younger, the Trotter family lived at this address in Peckham Rye.

8. The Hari Krishna temple is located here.

9. Dr Becker puts in a recommendation to the council that the Trotter family move to a new bungalow in this road.

10. The location of the fancy building where, according to Albert, 'all the young birds come out of at lunchtime'.

Answers

Around Peckham

1. Nelson Mandela House
2. Zimbabwe House
3. Walworth Road
4. King's Avenue
5. Tobacco Road
6. Desmond Tutu House
7. Peabody Buildings
8. Arnold Road
9. Herrington Road
10. Wilmot Road

Trotter Trivia

In addition to Dirty Barry's 'personal' shop, Walworth Road is also home to an all-night sandwich bar, as mentioned by policewoman Sandra in *Long Legs of the Law*.

Only Fools by Numbers

I've worked it out on the calculator, Rodney.

1. How many brothers does Denzil have?

2. According to Rodney, how many times has Del seen the film *Wall Street*?

3. In the episode *Chain Gang*, how many 24 carat gold chains does Arnie have for sale?

4. How many of these gold chains does Del initially offer to buy?

5. How many of Slater's illegally smuggled diamonds does Albert conceal in his pipe in *To Hull and Back*?

6. In the episode *As One Door Closes*, how many louvre doors does Del purchase from Teddy Cummings with the intention of selling on to Brendan O'Shaughnessy?

7. In which episode does Boycie utter the line "I didn't know you were good at maths, Del"?

8. In the very first episode *Big Brother*, how many dodgy briefcases does Del purchase from Trigger?

9. According to Del, how many Trotter chandeliers are there in Buckingham Palace?

10. Finally, one for die hard *Only Fools* fans - What is the six-digit combination of the briefcase that Boycie gives to Del in *To Hull and Back*?

Answers

Only Fools by Numbers

1. Five

2. Six

3. 250

4. Two

5. Two

6. 166

7. *A Losing Streak*

8. 25

9. Four

10. 714939

Trotter Trivia

In the episode *A Losing Streak,* as Del is explaining how he lost a bet to Boycie regarding what drink an Irish customer would order in The Nag's Head, he mentions 'the only genuine weightwatcher in London'. It's clear that the word 'genuine' has been dubbed on after shooting. The original line was 'the only Provo weightwatcher in London', a reference to the IRA which the BBC deemed unsuitable.

Only Fools and Geography

Let's leave Peckham for a moment and go further afield.

1. To which country did Del's former business partner Jumbo Mills emigrate?

2. In the very first episode *Big Brother*, after a disagreement with Del, Rodney tells Grandad he is going to hitchhike to where?

3. From which Dutch city do Del, Rodney and Albert smuggle diamonds for Boycie and Abdul?

4. To which country do Del and Rodney travel to attend Uncle Albert's war reunion?

5. Tom Clarke, Head of Security at Top Buy Superstores, once served in the police force of which African country?

6. Who encountered a 'man-eating' lion in the jungles of Africa when he was younger?

7. When Del is mistaken for a Mafia boss in *Miami Twice*, he finds himself negotiating a deal with two drug barons from which country?

8. In Rodney's dream sequence at the beginning of *Heroes and Villains*, a grown up and very powerful Damien is planning to go to war with which country?

9. What is the country of origin of the consignment of radio alarm clocks that go off 'any time they bloody like'?

10. In *Strangers on the Shore*, Del hires a van to drive Boycie to an important business meeting in which French city?

Answers

Only Fools and Geography

1. Australia

2. Hong Kong

3. Amsterdam

4. France

5. Kenya

6. Albert

7. Colombia

8. China

9. Latvia

10. Paris

Trotter Trivia

There have been a number of international versions of *Only Fools and Horses*, proving the show's worldwide appeal. The Netherlands was the first country to remake the show in 1995. A Portuguese version ran from 1999 to 2001, while a Slovenian remake from 2008 was made with the co-operation of John Sullivan himself.

Trotter A-Z – M and N

The answers to the first five clues all begin with M, while the final five answers all begin with N.

1. M – This flamenco-style double act provided the entertainment for the Spanish Night in The Nag's Head.

2. M – Trigger's female cousin who is a bit of a tomboy and enjoys smoking a pipe.

3. M – As a boy, Del's paper round took him to this road where he delivered a copy of Spick and Span to the 'weirdo' who lived there.

4. M – The brand of champagne that Del buys to celebrate Cassandra's pregnancy in *Modern Men*.

5. M – When he was younger, Rodney attempted to sell DIY gas conversion kits to the residents of this estate, not realising the properties were all-electric.

6. N – Directed by Mickey Pearce, this adult film was a production of the Boycie Video and Leisure Arts Company.

7. N – When sailing back from Holland, the Trotter boys decide to follow this ferry, only to discover it is going in the wrong direction.

8. N – Del and Rodney meet this girl, along with her friend Michelle, in the episode *Go West Young Man*.

9. N – Irene Mackay and her convict husband Tommy appear in this episode.

10. N – In *A Royal Flush*, Del initially believes that the Duke of Maylebury is a pub located in this area of Peckham.

Answers

Trotter A-Z – M and N

1. The Magaluf Brothers

2. Marilyn

3. Marley Road

4. Mont Chernobyl

5. Mountbatten Estate

6. Night Nurse

7. Norland

8. Nicky

9. No Greater Love

10. Nunhead

Trotter Trivia

Mentioned by Del in *Yuppy Love,* Spick and Span was a gentleman's 'glamour' magazine which featured models posing in their underwear. It ran from the fifties through to the mid-seventies.

The Best of John Sullivan

John Sullivan has written many classic TV programmes over the years. Can you identify some of his other work just by the programme initials and the years broadcast?

1. CS (1977-1980)

2. JGF (1983-1986)

3. DJ (1986-1987)

4. SP (1992-1993)

5. OH (1996)

6. HH (1998-2000)

7. M (2001-2002)

8. RR (1998-2003)

9. TGGG (2005-2009)

10. RAC (2010-2011)

Answers

The Best of John Sullivan

1. Citizen Smith

2. Just Good Friends

3. Dear John

4. Sitting Pretty

5. Over Here

6. Heartburn Hotel

7. Micawber

8. Roger Roger

9. The Green Green Grass

10. Rock and Chips

Trotter Trivia

In terms of viewing figures, *Just Good Friends* was John Sullivan's most successful sitcom outside of *Only Fools and Horses*. The 1986 Christmas special attracted 20.75 million viewers, making it one of the most-watched episodes of a British sitcom ever.

The Only Fools Soundtrack 2

The following songs have all featured on the soundtrack of various Only Fools and Horses episodes (titles in brackets). Can you name the artists for each one?

1. That Ole Devil Called Love (*The Unlucky Winner Is*)

2. True (*Rodney Come Home*)

3. Crocodile Rock (*Mother Nature's Son*)

4. Livin' La Vida Loca (*If They Could See Us Now*)

5. Sing (*Sleepless in Peckham*)

6. In the Summertime (*It Never Rains*)

7. Diane (*It's Only Rock and Roll*)

8. The Birdie Song (*The Unlucky Winner Is*)

9. So Macho (*The Frog's Legacy*)

10. Margate (*The Jolly Boys' Outing*)

Answers

The Only Fools Soundtrack 2

1. Alison Moyet

2. Spandau Ballet

3. Elton John

4. Ricky Martin

5. Travis

6. Mungo Jerry

7. The Bachelors

8. The Tweets

9. Sinitta

10. Chas and Dave

Trotter Trivia

The song *Margate* by Chas and Dave seemed like it was written especially for *The Jolly Boys' Outing*. However, the Cockney duo actually released the song seven years previously in 1982. The lyrics were slightly changed when featured on the end credits of *The Jolly Boys' Outing* and the voices of David Jason and Nicholas Lyndhurst were added.

Trotter A-Z – O and P

The answers to the first five clues all begin with O, while the final five answers all begin with P.

1. O - While on holiday in Miami, Del and Rodney are invited to stay at the plush residence of this Mafia family.

2. O - The vicar of the local church where Del witnesses the miracle which saves St Mary's Hospice.

3. O - This rather sad song about a dog is one of Del's personal favourites.

4. O - The burly doorman of the One Eleven Club who asks Rodney where he would 'like to land'.

5. O - The leader of a biker gang who is offered money by Del to 'sort out' the skinheads he thinks have mugged Albert.

6. P - Played by Jeff Stevenson, this police constable is seen working for Slater and Hoskins in *To Hull and Back*.

7. P - Although we never actually see her, this woman is supposedly the wife of crooked jewellery dealer and con man Arnie.

8. P - After receiving poor service from the cashier at Top Buy Superstore, Del mentions to Albert that from now on they will do their shopping at this convenience store.

9. P - The long-serving butler of the Duke of Maylebury in *A Royal Flush*.

10. P - Denzil originally wanted to call his courier business by this name before Del persuaded him otherwise.

Answers

Trotter A-Z – O and P

1. Occhetti

2. Father O'Keefe

3. Old Shep

4. Otto

5. Ollie

6. PC Parker

7. Pat

8. Patel's Multimart

9. Patterson

10. Peckham Courier Service

Trotter Trivia

Comic Jeff Stevenson is one of a handful of people who have played two different parts in *Only Fools and Horses*. In addition to PC Parker in *To Hull and Back*, Jeff was also the stand-up comedian who performed at Rodney's stag night in the series six episode *Little Problems* in 1989.

Only Fools in Cars

It's Top Gear, Peckham style!

1. What are the three place names featured on the side of the Trotter's van?

2. True or False – For the episode *Danger UXD*, writer John Sullivan originally considered blowing the Trotter van up?

3. In *Go West Young Man*, how much does Del pay Boycie for the clapped-out Ford Cortina?

4. In the same episode, what make of car do Del and Rodney end up looking after for Boycie?

5. What make of car does Del drive and later sell in the episode *Cash and Curry*?

6. In which episode does the green Ford Capri Ghia make its first appearance?

7. How much does Del pay Boycie for the Capri Ghia?

8. In *A Slow Bus to Chingford*, Del gets free use of a Leyland Bus for his new tourist venture. What does Del call this new enterprise?

9. Which character is seen driving a Jaguar XJ6 in the episode *Chain Gang*?

10. The blue Ford Transit van of which painter and decorator is seen parked outside the Nag's Head in *Who's a Pretty Boy?*

Answers

Only Fools in Cars

1. New York, Paris, Peckham

2. True

3. £25

4. E-Type Jaguar

5. Vauxhall Velox

6. He Ain't Heavy, He's My Uncle

7. £400

8. Trotter's Ethnic Tours

9. Arnie

10. Brendan O'Shaughnessy

Trotter Trivia

The legendary yellow three-wheeler belonging to the Trotters is often mistakenly referred to as a Reliant Robin. It is actually a Reliant Regal Supervan. Over the years, many different Supervans were used for filming.

Trotter A-Z – R and S

The answers to the first five clues all begin with R, while the final five answers all begin with S.

1. R – In *The Frog's Legacy*, Del is having trouble shifting this brand of computer.

2. R – Del, Rodney and Grandad manage to destroy a priceless chandelier at this stately home.

3. R – The name of Cassandra's pet rabbit which Rodney buys for her in *Heroes and Villains*.

4. R – The name of the head of security at the institute for the criminally insane in the episode *Friday the 14th*.

5. R – The surname of Tommy, the former Underground worker who went into business with Monkey Harris installing false ceilings.

6. S – The surname of Dougie, owner of a local stationery store who has a number of briefcases stolen from his premises.

7. S – Featured briefly in *Sleeping Dogs Lie*, we learn that this cute little dachshund has a tendency to chew carpets.

8. S – Del, Boycie and Abdul discuss the smuggling of diamonds while in the back of Denzil's lorry, which is parked outside a transport café in this road.

9. S – Along with Paddy the Greek, this unseen character stole lead from the church roof in *The Miracle of Peckham*.

10. S – The acronym for the Spa Water and Natural Spring Committee.

Answers

Trotter A-Z – R and S

1. Rajah Computers

2. Ridgemere Hall

3. Roger

4. Chief Robson

5. Razzle

6. Sadler

7. Sacha

8. Soweto Road

9. Sunglasses Ron

10. SWANS

Trotter Trivia

Christopher Malcolm, who memorably portrayed the crazed axeman in the episode *Friday the 14th* also appeared in the 1996 John Sullivan comedy drama *Over Here*. The late actor also enjoyed small roles in many Hollywood films such as *The Empire Strikes Back, Highlander, Spies Like Us* and *Labyrinth*.

Only Fools and Sport

The forgotten moments in sporting history...

1. According to Del, what is the nickname the press have bestowed upon Rodney due to his prowess on the international tennis circuit?

2. Which of Rodney's work colleagues believed that sugar diabetes was a Welsh flyweight?

3. After speedily running away from a mugger, Rodney is compared to which athlete by Del?

4. What was the outcome when Del got Boycie and his business client two tickets to Wimbledon?

5. According to Del, which footballer's free kicks are 'short and curly'?

6. What position did Monkey Harris play in the school football team?

7. Del and Rodney's mom Joan was a fan of which football team?

8. Del once sold a consignment of cricket bats which were supposedly autographed by which West Indies cricketing legend?

9. Who has 'been down more holes than Tony Jacklin' according to Del?

10. Del once set Rodney up with a girl who not only knew Zola Budd but was also the Southern Area Shot Put Champion. What was her name?

Answers

Only Fools and Sport

1. Hot Rod

2. Elvis

3. Linford Christie

4. They drew 0-0 with Ipswich

5. John Barnes

6. Left-back

7. Charlton Athletic

8. Viv Richards

9. Albert

10. Big Brenda

Trotter Trivia

Buster Merryfield was an accomplished boxer in his youth. In addition to being British champion as a schoolboy, Buster was the Southern Area Command champion during his time in the army.

Trotter A-Z – T and W

The answers to the first five clues all begin with T, while the final five answers all begin with W.

1. T – The cabaret club in Reading where Raquel gave her one and only solo singing performance.

2. T - In 1936, Grandad and his friend Nobby Clarke were imprisoned on the outskirts of this Spanish town.

3. T – The waiter at the Star of Bengal restaurant who serves Del in *Diamonds are for Heather* and *Healthy Competition*.

4. T - In Rodney's dream sequence in *Heroes and Villains*, this was the name of Del's airline.

5. T – The name of the security firm set up by Del in *A Slow Bus to Chingford*.

6. W – The surname of Spencer, the young man who is revealed to be the father of German student Anna's baby in *From Prussia with Love*.

7. W – Lord and Lady Ridgemere's faithful but aging butler.

8. W – The surname of Fatty, an old school friend of Del's who once sat on Slater's face while Trigger put itching powder in his belly button.

9. W - Although we never see this enthusiastic young police constable on screen, we learn from his experienced partner Eric that he is on the lookout for his first 'nick'.

10. W – Surname of Richard, the real-life news anchor who had a cameo role as a newsreader in *The Sky's the Limit*.

Answers

Trotter A-Z – T and W

1. Talk of the Town
2. Tarifa
3. Tony
4. Trotter Air
5. Trotter Watch
6. Wainwright
7. Wallace
8. Walker
9. Wayne
10. Whitmore

Trotter Trivia

In addition to appearing on screen presenting the news in *The Sky's the Limit*, Richard Whitmore's voice can be heard reading the TV news report concerning the contaminated water supplies in the 1992 special *Mother Nature's Son*.

Unseen Characters

The following are all names of unseen characters in Only Fools and Horses which have had alternate letters removed. Can you work out who they are?

1. M_N_E_ H_R_I_

2. P_D_Y _H_ G_E_K

3. L_M_Y _I_N_L

4. U_A_D_N _O_R_S

5. R_N_I_ N_L_O_

6. S_N_L_S_E_ R_N

7. A_F_E _L_W_R_

8. T_M_Y R_Z_L_

9. L_N_Y N_R_I_

10. G_N_E_ T_D

Answers

Unseen Characters

1. Monkey Harris
2. Paddy the Greek
3. Limpy Lionel
4. Ugandan Morris
5. Ronnie Nelson
6. Sunglasses Ron
7. Alfie Flowers
8. Tommy Razzle
9. Lenny Norris
10. Ginger Ted

Trotter Trivia

Perhaps the most well-remembered of the unseen characters, Monkey Harris was first mentioned in the episode *The Long Legs of the Law* as Del explains to Grandad about Monkey's new business partnership with the also unseen Tommy Razzle.

Who's Rachel? Part 2

The following quotes from the series all have the names of famous people missing from them. Can you fill in the blanks?

1. He's sucking the land dry! I'm worried we're going to get a visit from Bob Geldof and BLANK any minute! (*Rodney*)

2. How can bloody Linda Evans be BLANK? (*Rodney*)

3. With the money you could earn out of this, you could have that place reopened, redecorated and get BLANK to open it for you. (*Del*)

4. I stole it off him Rodders! 400 nicker! It's a peach – handles better than BLANK. (*Del*)

5. Who in their right mind would call their place the Hotel BLANK? (*Rodney*)

6. That's Derek Trotter in there, not bloody BLANK! (*Denzil*)

7. A bottle of that Dillinger's 75. That's BLANK'S favourite champagne that. (*Del*)

8. Well, I wondered why Sidney Potter kept bursting into song. I don't like BLANK (*Grandad*)

9. Russell Crowe? You look like BLANK with piles. (*Del*)

10. Del had more fights than BLANK. (*Grandad*)

Answers

Who's Rachel? Part 2

1. Lenny Henry

2. Joan Collins

3. Samantha Fox

4. Maradona

5. Hitler

6. Einstein

7. Prince Charles

8. Harry Belafonte

9. Spartacus

10. John Wayne

Trotter Trivia

Harry Belafonte was mentioned at the beginning of *Big Brother*, the very first episode of *Only Fools and Horses*, with Grandad mistaking the singer for actor Sidney Poitier.

Only Fools and Horses Work

Here's a job-lot of work-related questions for you.

1. According to Del, Mickey Pearce only became a vegetarian after getting the sack from which establishment?

2. Who took over as the Head of the Computer Section at Parry Printing after Rodney's resignation?

3. In which industry does Cassandra work?

4. After being released from prison which disgraced former police officer got a job working for an undertaker in Colchester?

5. Which Peckham resident was made redundant in the episode *As One Door Closes*?

6. Which mathematical term did Del's dad Reg once try to use as an excuse for having time off sick from work?

7. Before making an unwelcome return home at Christmas in *Thicker than Water*, Reg had been working as a porter at which hospital?

8. Which familiar face from The Nag's Head once worked as a cocktail waiter on a cruise ship?

9. In *A Slow Bus to Chingford*, Rodney is employed as an NSO by Del's new venture Trotter Watch. What do the initials NSO stand for?

10. Which of Rodney's friends works as a ladies' hairstylist?

Answers

Only Fools and Horses Work

1. World of Leather

2. Elvis

3. Banking

4. Slater

5. Denzil

6. Cubic foot

7. Newcastle Infirmary

8. Mike

9. Nocturnal Security Officer

10. Chris

Trotter Trivia

Before his career as a writer took off, John Sullivan worked in a number of different jobs including stints cleaning windows, stacking crates in a brewery and laying carpets in the House of Commons. Eventually he found himself working as a scene shifter in the comedy department at the BBC. After mentioning an idea for a new comedy series to producer Dennis Main Wilson, John took two weeks off and wrote the script for his first hit, *Citizen Smith*.

Only Fools and Opposites

Can you work out the titles of the Only Fools and Horses episodes from these alternative 'opposite' titles?

1. Small Sister

2. The Shortest Day

3. Come East Old Woman

4. Health and Poverty

5. The Lucky Loser Isn't

6. Villains and Heroes

7. Waking Cats Sit

8. Tomorrow Always Arrives

9. The Americans are Going

10. As Two Windows Open

11. Shorts Arms of the Criminals

12. It Always Shines

13. Who Isn't An Ugly Girl?

14. Listening to the Boys Come By

15. Sad Deliveries

Answers

Only Fools and Opposites

1. Big Brother
2. The Longest Night
3. Go West Young Man
4. Sickness and Wealth
5. The Unlucky Winner Is
6. Heroes and Villains
7. Sleeping Dogs Lie
8. Yesterday Never Comes
9. The Russians are Coming
10. As One Door Closes
11. Long Legs of the Law
12. It Never Rains
13. Who's a Pretty Boy?
14. Watching the Girls Go By
15. Happy Returns

Trotter Trivia

Happy Returns was one of two extra episodes in series four that John Sullivan had to write in order to explain the absence of Grandad. Lennard Pearce had sadly passed away just after filming on the new series began.

Only Fools in One Word

Can you guess the titles of Only Fools and Horses episodes from just one relevant word?

1. Canary

2. Butterfly

3. Microwave

4. Margate

5. Chandelier

6. Batman

7. Holland

8. Seance

9. Cwying

10. Urn

11. Luminous

12. Shadow

13. Mafia

14. Vasectomy

15. Gary

Answers

Only Fools in One Word

1. Who's a Pretty Boy?

2. As One Door Closes

3. May the Force Be With You

4. The Jolly Boys' Outing

5. A Touch of Glass

6. Heroes and Villains

7. To Hull and Back

8. Sickness and Wealth

9. Stage Fright

10. Ashes to Ashes

11. The Yellow Peril

12. The Longest Night

13. Miami Twice

14. Modern Men

15. Strangers on the Shore

Trotter Trivia

The Jamaican Swallowtail butterfly, which Del and Rodney try to catch in *As One Door Closes*, is the largest species of butterfly in the Western Hemisphere with an average wingspan of 6 inches. The species is, sadly, critically endangered.

Name the Only Fools Star

*Each question features four television shows that a
particular star of Only Fools and Horses has appeared in.
There are ten different stars to guess.*

1. *Still Open All Hours, A Bit of a Do, Lucky Feller, Porridge.*

2. *Benidorm, The Green Green Grass, Doctor Who, Citizen
Smith.*

3. *Going Straight, Rock and Chips, Butterflies, The Two of
Us.*

4. *The Green Green Grass, Still Open All Hours, Dear John,
Doctors.*

5. *EastEnders, Lucy Sullivan is Getting Married, A Touch of
Frost, Real Women.*

6. *The Old Guys, Hustle, 2 Point 4 Children, The Vicar of
Dibley.*

7. *The Dick Emery Show, It Ain't Half Hot Mum, Crocodile
Shoes II, David Copperfield.*

8. *Minder, Hammer House of Horror, Dr Finlay's Case Book,
Shroud for a Nightingale.*

9. *So Haunt Me, The Demon Headmaster, Holby City,
Grantchester.*

10. *Game of Thrones, The Peter Principle, Happy Families,
Blackadder's Christmas Carol.*

Answers

Name the Only Fools Star

1. David Jason
2. John Challis
3. Nicholas Lyndhurst
4. Sue Holderness
5. Gwyneth Strong
6. Roger Lloyd Pack
7. Kenneth MacDonald
8. Lennard Pearce
9. Tessa Peake-Jones
10. Jim Broadbent

Trotter Trivia

Like her on-screen husband Nicholas Lyndhurst, Gwyneth Strong started her career as a child star. She made her debut aged just thirteen in the 1973 horror film *Nothing But the Night*, which starred Christopher Lee and Peter Cushing.

Only Fools and TV

Each of these lines of dialogue has the name of a television show in initials. Can you name the show for each one?

1. I doubt he'd want to go with you anyway, he's watching **TOTP** on the portable.

2. I'm trying to get **TDOH**.

3. No, not **D**. Definitely not **D**.

4. There's no danger of him winning **B** though is there?

5. Oh, I thought you meant **TMD**. Marlene and Duke sit and watch that. Soppy as sacks the two of 'em. The dog gets more questions right than her.

6. I asked him to set this to record a programme on ITV called city news. What have I got? **OU** on BBC2.

7. If you watch an episode of **B** and Little Joe falls in love with a woman, you know she is going to die.

8. I just got up to switch over to **C**.

9. A mug of Bournvita, plate of toast and **MOTD**, that's us, eh, Rodders?

10. Yes, thank you Rodney. Could we leave **TIYL** to Michael Aspel?

Answers

Only Fools and TV

1. Top of the Pops
2. The Dukes of Hazzard
3. Dallas
4. Blockbusters
5. That's My Dog
6. Open University
7. Bonanza
8. Crossroads
9. Match of the Day
10. This is Your Life

Trotter Trivia

One of David Jason's very first television roles was in the long-running ITV soap opera *Crossroads*. He joined the show in 1967 but was only there for a short time.

Only Fools Last Words

Can you name the episodes from which the following pieces of dialogue are the last lines?

1. Put that round your Gucci! It'll stop your sole coming off!

2. Make sure you don't take the shortcut across the railway line.

3. I'm gonna stick this right up your jacksie!

4. So, she was engaged all the time. What a couple of wallies!

5. Switch it off!

6. I wouldn't mind betting that this time next week my name will be in all the papers.

7. You'll give yourself a heart attack.

8. Trigger's gran was married twice! Oh no!

9. Welcome home boys.

10. This time next year we'll be billionaires!

Answers

Only Fools Last Words

1. Healthy Competition
2. Happy Returns
3. It's Only Rock and Roll
4. Tea for Three
5. The Sky's the Limit
6. Mother Nature's Son
7. Chain Gang
8. Ashes to Ashes
9. Miami Twice
10. Time on Our Hands

Trotter Trivia

First broadcast on 29 December 1996, the episode *Time on Our Hands* is the most watched programme in British television history, pulling in an astonishing 24.3 million viewers. This is a record that will likely never be broken.

Episode Guide

Facts and Figures

First Episode Broadcast: 8 September 1981

Last Episode Broadcast: 25 December 2003

Number of Episodes: 64

Number of Series: 7

Number of Christmas Specials: 18

First Feature Length Episode: To Hull and Back (25 Dec 85)

Final Episode with Grandad: Thicker Than Water (25 Dec 83)

First Episode with Uncle Albert: Strained Relations (28 Feb 85)

Final 30 Min Episode: Who Wants to be a Millionaire? (5 Oct 86)

First 50 Min Episode: Yuppy Love (8 Jan 89)

Series 1 Episode 1

Big Brother

Broadcast Date: 8 September 1981

Audience Figure: 9.2 million

Synopsis: On our first ever visit to Nelson Mandela House, there seems to be a little bit of tension between brothers Del and Rodney. Older sibling Del is keen to make a deal with mate Trigger for twenty-five 'old English vinyl' briefcases, while Rodney, the new financial adviser for Trotters Independent Traders, remains sceptical. Ignoring his brothers concerns, Del buys the briefcases only to discover this particular batch has a major flaw concerning the combination locks. To add to his troubles, Del has to mount a search for Rodney who, after feeling his worth to the firm has been underestimated, has decided to run away to Hong Kong.

Starring: David Jason, Nicholas Lyndhurst, Lennard Pearce, Roger Lloyd Pack, Peta Barnard.

Trotter Trivia: Along with David Jason and Nicholas Lyndhurst, Roger Lloyd Pack was one of only three people from this first episode who also appeared in the final episode in 2003.

Series 1 Episode 2

Go West Young Man

Broadcast Date: 15 September 1981

Audience Figure: 6.1 million

Synopsis: Del is looking to diversify. As he enthusiastically explains to Rodney, "Britain's future lies fairly and squarely in the second-hand car game." It looks like a visit to Del's old school mate Boycie, who runs a second-hand car business, is in order. While Del has his eye on a rust-infested Mark II

Cortina with bald tyres, Boycie shows off a stunning E-Type Jaguar which he intends to give to his 'bit on the side' as a birthday present. Needing to keep the car out of sight of wife Marlene, Boycie reluctantly agrees to Del hiding it in his garage, selling him the Cortina for a knock-down price in return.

Starring: David Jason, Nicholas Lyndhurst, Lennard Pearce, John Challis, Nick Stringer, JoAnne Good, Caroline Ellis.

Trotter Trivia: This episode features the debut of second-hand car dealer Boycie, played with relish by the wonderful John Challis.

Series 1 Episode 3
Cash and Curry

Broadcast Date: 22 September 1981

Audience Figure: 7.3 million

Synopsis: Del has made a new contact in the business world, a personable and very wealthy man named Vimmal Malik. Upon leaving a business function together, Del and Vimmal are confronted by another businessman who identifies himself as Mr Ram, a long-time rival to Vimmal. For many years, the families of the two men have been feuding over the ownership of a priceless statue. With custom declaring that neither man can communicate with the other, can Del engineer a deal between the rivals over the statue and make a tidy profit for himself into the bargain?

Starring: David Jason, Nicholas Lyndhurst, Ahmed Khalil, Renu Setna, Babar Bhatti.

Trotter Trivia: Although Grandad is mentioned a couple of times, Lennard Pearce does not actually appear in this episode.

Series 1 Episode 4
The Second Time Around

Broadcast Date: 29 September 1981

Audience Figure: 7.8 million

Synopsis: Popping into The Nag's Head for a quick drink during a busy day at the market, Del is surprised to come across Pauline Harris, an old flame from many years ago. In a matter of moments Del begins to fall for the charms of Pauline all over again, despite his former girlfriend having buried a number of husbands in the intervening years. It isn't long before Pauline has moved into the flat at Nelson Mandela House, leading to a disgruntled Grandad and Rodney announcing that they are going to stay with Auntie Rose in Clacton.

Starring: David Jason, Nicholas Lyndhurst, Lennard Pearce, Roger Lloyd Pack, Jill Baker, Beryl Cooke, Peta Barnard.

Series 1 Episode 5
A Slow Bus to Chingford

Broadcast Date: 6 October 1981

Audience Figure: 7 million

Synopsis: Del decides to enter the security business. Trotter Watch, a subsidiary of Trotter's Independent Traders, is duly launched and the very first employee of this exciting new venture is a rather reluctant Rodney. Del informs his brother that his new job title is NCO or 'Nocturnal Security Officer'. The younger Trotter is required to keep an overnight watch at the local bus station, at first completely unaware that Del has set this deal up in order to gain use of a double decker bus in return. Del needs such a vehicle for his other new venture, a tour company called Trotter's Ethnic Tours.

Starring: David Jason, Nicholas Lyndhurst, Lennard Pearce, Gaynor Ward.

Series 1 Episode 6
The Russians are Coming

Broadcast Date: 13 October 1981

Audience Figure: 8.8 million

Synopsis: Rodney is distinctly unimpressed with Del's latest purchase, a seemingly useless pile of bricks and rubble. However, his interest is peaked somewhat when Del shows him what lies underneath – a large quantity of lead. Knowing the huge price that lead fetches on the open market, Del is keen to sell as soon as possible. However, Rodney discovers a set of instructions with the lead, revealing that the metal is part of a do-it-yourself air raid shelter kit.

Starring: David Jason, Nicholas Lyndhurst, Lennard Pearce, Derek Newark.

Trotter Trivia: The Russians are Coming was second only to *Big Brother* in terms of audience figures for series one.

Series 1 Episode 7 – Christmas Special
Christmas Crackers

Broadcast Date: 28 December 1981

Audience Figure: 7.5 million

Synopsis: The festive season sees Del and Rodney once again facing the prospect of Grandad cooking Christmas dinner. Rodney is in a rebellious mood and wants to go on a hunger strike in order to avoid the inevitable culinary disaster but Del explains how cooking the Christmas dinner every year makes Grandad feel like he has an important role to play in the family. However, this doesn't make the incinerated roast potatoes and strained gravy taste any better or change the fact that the plastic bag containing the giblets has been left inside the cooked turkey.

Starring: David Jason, Nicholas Lyndhurst, Lennard Pearce, Desmond McNamara.

Trotter Trivia: This is the only episode of the first five series not to be produced by Ray Butt.

Series 2 Episode 1

Long Legs of the Law

Broadcast Date: 21 October 1982

Audience Figure: 7.7 million

Synopsis: It is the morning after a double date night for Del and Rodney and the younger Trotter is not happy. After all, when Del told him they were going on a double date with a mother and a daughter, Rodney assumed (wrongly) that he would be with the daughter. Del recounts the story of the evening to Grandad, revealing how a huge fight broke out between business partners Monkey Harris and Tommy Razzle, leading to a lone policewoman being sent to deal with the matter. At first laughing off Rodney's lame attempts at trying to gain a date with the policewoman while she was attempting an arrest, Del is horrified to learn that his brother's chat-up technique worked and the young officer has agreed to a date with Rodney.

Starring: David Jason, Nicholas Lyndhurst, Lennard Pearce, Kate Saunders

Trotter Trivia: Café owner Sid makes his first appearance in this episode.

Series 2 Episode 2

Ashes to Ashes

Broadcast Date: 28 October 1982

Audience Figure: 9.8 million

Synopsis: It is a sad for Trigger as his grandmother Alice has passed away. Upon learning that Trigger will be the only mourner at the funeral, Del and Rodney decide to go along to pay their respects too. They are joined by Grandad, who had been good friends with Alice in their younger days. Gathering at Alice's house to await the funeral car, Trigger explains to the group how Alice had an affair with another man while his grandad Arthur was away fighting in the war. Del is more interested in a pair of Meissen urns residing in the living room, which he persuades Trigger to let him take in order to sell on his behalf. Back at Nelson Mandela House, Grandad is horrified to find Arthur's ashes in one of the urns and reveals to Del and Rodney that it was he who had the affair with Alice.

Starring: David Jason, Nicholas Lyndhurst, Lennard Pearce, Roger Lloyd Pack

Trotter Trivia: John D. Collins, who has a brief role as a river policeman in this episode, also played the vet who treats Duke in the series four episode *Sleeping Dogs Lie.*

Series 2 Episode 3

A Losing Streak

Broadcast Date: 4 November 1982

Audience Figure: 7.5 million

Synopsis: Del is in the middle of a gambling losing streak, continually losing money in card games. To make matters worse, the majority of that money is being lost to Boycie, who is delighting in rubbing salt into Del's wounds. Looking to help Del recoup some losses, Grandad gives Del a double-headed coin that a deserter gave to him during the war. Armed with the coin, Del visits the Nag's Head to arrange another poker game with Boycie, much to Rodney's chagrin. After losing a bet over a drinks order, Del tries to recoup the money with a coin toss. Unfortunately, Boycie calls heads. Ever the optimist, Del still believes that he can snap his losing streak and arranges a big poker game with Boycie and Trigger at Nelson Mandela House that evening.

Starring: David Jason, Nicholas Lyndhurst, Lennard Pearce, Roger Lloyd Pack, John Challis

Series 2 Episode 4

No Greater Love

Broadcast Date: 11 November 1982

Audience Figure: 8.6 million

Synopsis: The Trotters are now selling their wares door to door with customers able to make weekly payments. Del sends Rodney to collect monies owed by Mrs Singh but it transpires that she has left the area. Irene Mackay has taken over the flat and it isn't long before Rodney is smitten with the older newcomer, despite there being a considerable age gap between the two. Even the fact that Irene's husband Tommy is serving time in Parkhurst for GBH and attempted murder doesn't deter the love-struck Trotter from striking up a relationship. Will the fact that Tommy is due for parole very soon help to change Rodney's mind?

Starring: David Jason, Nicholas Lyndhurst, Lennard Pearce, David Daker, Gaye Brown.

Series 2 Episode 5
The Yellow Peril

Broadcast Date: 18 November 1982

Audience Figure: 8.2 million

Synopsis: Del is keen on entering the painting and decorating game and spots an opportunity to do just that when the local Chinese takeaway is tipped off by a mysterious anonymous caller that the local health inspector is due to pay a visit. Del is pleased to land the job as this means he can shift the numerous tins of yellow paint that he has bought cheaply from Trigger. With Rodney as the painter and Grandad as the apprentice, the kitchen of the Golden Lotus is soon freshly painted. It all seems to be a job well done until Trigger reveals that the paint is not only stolen property but is also mainly used to paint signs in railway tunnels, meaning it is, in fact, luminous.

Starring: David Jason, Nicholas Lyndhurst, Lennard Pearce, Roger Lloyd Pack, Rex Wei.

Series 2 Episode 6
It Never Rains

Broadcast Date: 25 November 1982

Audience Figure: 9.5 million

Synopsis: It has been raining non-stop in Peckham for days, not ideal when you have a consignment of Italian sun hats for sale. Taking shelter in The Nag's Head, Del bumps into Alex, owner of the local travel agent. Struggling for business, Alex is looking for ideas on how he can boost trade. With his ever keen eye for a potential bargain, Del suggests a once in a lifetime offer of 80% off the price of a holiday anywhere in the world but only to the next customer who enters Alex's shop.

With Del securing an 80% reduction deal with Alex, the Trotter brothers have the entire world at their disposal and decide to go somewhere different to the normal tourist hotspots, namely Benidorm. After initially booking for just two people, Grandad is soon added to the holiday party and the Trotters are off to sunny Spain. The only potential snag is the fact that Grandad has been on Spanish shores before and may not exactly be welcomed back with open arms.

Starring: David Jason, Nicholas Lyndhurst, Lennard Pearce, Jim McManus, Antony Jackson.

Trotter Trivia: Studland Bay in Dorset stood in for the beach in Benidorm for the filming of this episode.

Series 2 Episode 7

A Touch of Glass

Broadcast Date: 2 December 1982

Audience Figure: 10.2 million

Synopsis: Del, Rodney and Grandad are returning from a successful trip to an auction when they come across a lady whose car has broken down in a country lane, Del is quick to offer the use of Grandad's scarf to tow the vehicle back to the lady's residence when he finds out that she is Lady Ridgemere of Ridgemere Hall. After talking his way inside the stately home, Del overhears Lord Ridgemere haggling on the telephone over the price of chandelier maintenance. What a pity that his Lordship doesn't realise the Trotter family are renowned experts in the field of chandelier cleaning and repair. The two priceless Louis XIV chandeliers hanging in Ridgemere Hall shouldn't present too much of a challenge, even with Grandad undoing the bolts.

Starring: David Jason, Nicholas Lyndhurst, Lennard Pearce, Geoffrey Toone, Elizabeth Benson, Donald Bisset.

Series 2 Christmas Special

Diamonds Are for Heather

Broadcast Date: 30 December 1982

Audience Figure: 9.3 million

Synopsis: It's Spanish Night in The Nag's Head and even the musical delights of The Magaluf Brothers cannot cheer Del up. Recently he has been rather unlucky in love and the only song he wants to hear right now is *Old Shep*. The downbeat song empties the pub, save for a pretty girl at the bar called Heather. Del strikes up a conversation with the lovely newcomer and soon the two become inseparable. With Christmas on the horizon, Del is in a giving mood. Specifically he is planning to give Heather an engagement ring but the reappearance of Heather's estranged husband may yet spoil Del's surprise.

Starring: David Jason, Nicholas Lyndhurst, Lennard Pearce, Rosalind Lloyd

Trotter Trivia: This episode is famous for featuring the song *Zoom*, which was a number 2 hit in the UK singles chart for Fat Larry's Band in October 1982.

Series 3 Episode 1

Homesick

Broadcast Date: 10 November 1983

Audience Figure: 9.4 million

Synopsis: With the lifts in Nelson Mandela House broken down once again, Rodney is hoping he can put his position on the local Tenant's Association to good use by rectifying the situation. The meeting doesn't quite go as Rodney planned, as the younger Trotter finds himself thrust into the position of Association Chairman. When Grandad collapses due to the exertion of climbing the many flights of stairs in Nelson

Mandela House, Del is sure that Rodney will do the right thing for the family and use his sway as Chairman of the Tenant's Association to ensure the Trotters are moved to one of the new council bungalows in Herrington Road.

Starring: David Jason, Nicholas Lyndhurst, Lennard Pearce, Sandra Payne, John Bryans, Ron Pember.

Trotter Trivia: Homesick was the first episode in which Rodney challenged Trigger as to why he continually called him Dave.

Series 3 Episode 2

Healthy Competition

Broadcast Date: 17 November 1983

Audience Figure: 9.7 million

Synopsis: Rodney's less than enthusiastic approach to his job as Trotter's Independent Trader's official look-out leads to Del being chased through the back streets of Peckham by not only the police but also an energetic pack of stray dogs. Putting his lack of concentration down to having other things on his mind, Rodney announces he is leaving the Trotter partnership in order to go it alone...well, alone if you don't count Mickey Pearce as financial director anyway. While Mickey's mum is soon receiving a postcard from her son all the way from Benidorm, Rodney is finding it difficult to keep the fledgling business afloat. If only he could find a buyer for that job lot of broken lawnmower engines he and Mickey bought from the auction a few weeks ago.

Starring: David Jason, Nicholas Lyndhurst, Lennard Pearce, Patrick Murray.

Trotter Trivia: Although the character of Mickey Pearce had been mentioned in previous episodes, this was the first time he was actually seen on-screen.

Series 3 Episode 3
Friday the 14th

Broadcast Date: 24 November 1983

Audience Figure: 9.7 million

Synopsis: Del has entered into a temporary business arrangement with Boycie. Agreeing to supply Mario's restaurant with a supply of fresh salmon, Del, Rodney and Grandad are offered the use of Boycie's holiday cottage in Cornwall for a weekend of fishing (make that poaching). Arriving at their destination in the middle of a heavy storm which has caused a blackout in the area, the Trotters are warned by a local policeman to be on their guard as an inmate from an insane asylum has escaped and is still believed to be in the immediate vicinity. With a reluctant Rodney and Grandad in tow, Del is determined to go through with his plan. After all, there is a tenner per fish at stake here.

Starring: David Jason, Nicholas Lyndhurst, Lennard Pearce, Christopher Malcolm, Ray Mort.

Series 3 Episode 4
Yesterday Never Comes

Broadcast Date: 1 December 1983

Audience Figure: 10.6 Million

Synopsis: Never one to shirk a challenge, Del ploughs headlong into the specialist world of antiques. His first acquisition is a genuine Queen Anne cabinet which Del hopes to sell for ninety-five. Grandad wonders why Del doesn't go the whole hog and charge a pound. Their first interested party is upmarket Chelsea antiques dealer Miranda Davenport. The fact that the cabinet is an obvious fake doesn't seem to worry Miranda that much. Instead, she seems to have fallen for the charms of Del himself. Could the well-to-do Miranda really be infatuated with market trader Del or has a certain painting hanging on the wall in the Trotter flat caught her eye instead?

Starring: David Jason, Nicholas Lyndhurst, Lennard Pearce, Juliet Hammond-Hill.

Series 3 Episode 5

May the Force Be With You

Broadcast Date: 8 December 1983

Audience Figure: 10.7 million

Synopsis: While Grandad is busy trying to tune a microwave oven into the latest episode of *The Dukes of Hazzard,* Rodney is in The Nag's Head where he bumps into Trigger, Boycie and an old school acquaintance of theirs, Roy Slater. Believing that Del will be overjoyed to meet an old school friend after all these years, Rodney invites Slater back to the flat, much, it turns out, to Del's horror. As Del Boy hurriedly explains to Rodney, Slater is a Detective Inspector in the police force and he doesn't let sentimentality get in the way of an arrest. The ambitious copper is on the look-out for a stolen microwave oven, one that looks remarkably like the one in the Trotter flat. With all three Trotters arrested for receiving stolen goods, it seems that Slater has finally got one over his old adversary from school.

Starring: David Jason, Nicholas Lyndhurst, Lennard Pearce, Roger Lloyd Pack, John Challis, Jim Broadbent, Christopher Mitchell.

Trotter Trivia: This episode saw the first on-screen appearance of Del's old school friend turned enemy, Roy Slater.

Series 3 Episode 6
Wanted

Broadcast Date: 15 December 1983

Audience Figure: 11.2 million

Synopsis: Walking home after a night in The Nag's Head, Rodney comes across an inebriated woman who seems to be in distress. Ever the gentleman, Rodney puts a hand out to steady the woman as she staggers, which leads to her accusing him of assault. Wracked with worry, Rodney recounts the evening's events to Del and Grandad the next morning. As Rodney tells his story, Del quickly realises the woman in question is Blossom, an eccentric local character who is known to the police for falsely reporting incidents such as this. Spying a golden opportunity to wind his younger brother up, Del keeps quiet about his knowledge of Blossom and soon has Rodney believing he is a wanted man, leading to the younger Trotter going on the run.

Starring: David Jason, Nicholas Lyndhurst, Lennard Pearce, Roger Lloyd Pack, John Challis, Patrick Murray.

Series 3 Episode 7
Who's a Pretty Boy?

Broadcast Date: 22 December 1983

Audience Figure: 11.9 million

Synopsis: Despite the disastrous painting of the Chinese takeaway kitchen a while back, Del is keen to get back into the decorating game, especially when he hears that old rival Brendan O'Shaughnessy has just landed the job of redecorating Denzil's flat. Desperate to get one over the Irish decorator, Del talks his old schoolmate Denzil into letting the Trotters do the job instead, despite strong protestations from Denzil's formidable wife Corrine. While Grandad makes a hole in the Jaffa Cakes on their first day decorating, Rodney

117

manages to make a hole in the bottom of the kettle. Worse still, Corrine's beloved canary Sylvester is looking exceedingly lifeless in the bottom of his cage. How is Del going to talk his way out of this one?

Starring: David Jason, Nicholas Lyndhurst, Lennard Pearce, Paul Barber, Kenneth MacDonald, David Jackson, Eva Mottley.

Trotter Trivia: This episode saw the debuts of two characters who would go on to become much loved *Only Fools & Horses* regulars – Denzil and Mike.

Series 3 Christmas Special

Thicker Than Water

Broadcast Date: 25 December 1983

Audience Figure: 10.8 million

Synopsis: The Christmas season never seems to run smoothly for the Trotters. As Del points out, "Some people get wise men bearing gifts. We get a wally with a disease!" The wally in question is Del and Rodney's estranged father Reg, who turns up on the doorstep on Christmas night. While Grandad is pleased to see his son and Rodney is keen to get to know his father, Del is unhappy that Reg has surfaced once more. Remembering how he walked out on the family many years ago, Del's feelings towards his father only begin to soften when he hears that Reg is suffering from a rare blood disorder. As the disorder is hereditary, Del and Rodney each take a blood test. Although the tests come back negative, another issue threatens to throw a huge cloud over the Trotter's Christmas as the results reveal that the Trotter brothers have different blood groups. Could Del or Rodney have been fathered by another man?

Starring: David Jason, Nicholas Lyndhurst, Lennard Pearce, Peter Woodthorpe.

Trotter Trivia: This was the last regular *Only Fools and Horses* episode to feature Lennard Pearce as Grandad.

(Image Copyright: British Broadcasting Corporation)

Series 4 Episode 1

Happy Returns

Broadcast Date: 21 February 1985

Audience Figure: 15.2 million

Synopsis: Rodney is smitten by Debbie, a girl who works in the local newsagents. Despite Del's best efforts to embarrass him, Rodney manages to get a date with the object of his affection. Meanwhile, Del comes across a young boy out in the street on his own after dark. Concerned for his safety, Del escorts the boy back home to his mum and is amazed to find out that the mum is actually an old flame of his, June Snell. June is also the mother of Debbie, Rodney's girlfriend from the newsagents. Rekindling their relationship from nearly twenty years before, Del and June get into a discussion over why June suddenly left Del without explanation. While June refuses to reveal the reason why she left, Del is left working things out on a calculator when he finds out that June's daughter Debbie is soon to turn nineteen and he and June broke up nineteen and a half years ago...

Starring: David Jason, Nicholas Lyndhurst, Roger Lloyd Pack, Patrick Murray, Diane Langton, Oona Kirsch.

Trotter Trivia: The original opening episode to series four was scheduled to be *Hole in One* but the death of Lennard Pearce meant plans had to change and John Sullivan penned two extra episodes to write Grandad out of the series and introduce his long lost brother, the old sea dog Uncle Albert.

Series 4 Episode 2

Strained Relations

Broadcast Date: 28 February 1985

Audience Figure: 14.9 million

Synopsis: Grandad has passed on and both Del and Rodney are struggling to cope with their loss. Grandad's funeral sees members of the Trotter family from North London attend, including Grandad's estranged younger brother Albert, a former Navy man. Albert attends the funeral with Del's cousin Stan and his wife Jean, with whom Albert has been living for the past few years. Spying an opportunity to be rid of the old sea dog, Stan and Jean leave Albert at the Trotter flat and drive off in their caravan. While Del is not initially keen on Albert staying with them, preferring he get a bed at the local seaman's mission, those irresistible family ties may yet mean the Trotter flat will once again have three inhabitants.

Starring: David Jason, Nicholas Lyndhurst, Buster Merryfield, Roger Lloyd Pack, John Challis, Kenneth MacDonald.

Trotter Trivia: This episode features the very first appearance of Buster Merryfield as Uncle Albert.

Series 4 Episode 3
Hole in One

Broadcast Date: 7 March 1985

Audience Figure: 13.4 million

Synopsis: Winter has descended on Peckham, with a hard frost covering the ground and a chill wind that, according to Albert, 'cuts right through you'. Del believes it is the 'worst winter in over two million years', so is understandably perplexed and not a little angry that Rodney has spent the last of the firm's remaining capital on a £500 job lot of suntan lotion. With zero capital and no suitable stock to trade with, Trotter's Independent Traders is in trouble. Uncle Albert's reassurances to Del that something will turn up prove accurate when the old sea dog falls down the cellar of The Nag's Head. Del is determined to claim compensation for his uncle's accident, so the firm's solicitor Solly Atwell is duly called into action.

Starring: David Jason, Nicholas Lyndhurst, Buster Merryfield, Kenneth MacDonald, Colin Jeavons, Nula Conwell.

Trotter Trivia: Some location scenes featuring Lennard Pearce outside of the court in the wheelchair were shot before filming was cancelled due to Lennard's death in December 1984.

Series 4 Episode 4
It's Only Rock and Roll

Broadcast Date: 14 March 1985

Audience Figure: 13.6 Million

Synopsis: Rodney is the drummer in a local band who are aiming to style themselves on Frankie Goes to Hollywood. Unfortunately the band's equipment is sorely lacking, with instruments consisting of two acoustic guitars and a couple of wooden packing crates substituting for drums. On top of that, the lead singer is 'Mental' Mickey McGuire, a decidedly unstable individual who vehemently insists on doing the 'one, two, three, fours...' What the band needs is a manager to guide them, a role which Del volunteers himself for. Does a previously sceptical Del Boy really believe A Bunch of Wallies has what it takes to make it in the pop world or has his sudden change of heart been brought about by the news that The Shamrock Club are without a band for St Patrick's Night?

Starring: David Jason, Nicholas Lyndhurst, Buster Merryfield, Daniel Peacock, David Thewlis.

Series 4 Episode 5

Sleeping Dogs Lie

Broadcast Date: 21 March 1985

Audience Figure: 18.7 million

Synopsis: Del is in a happy mood as he has just pulled off a 'genuine coup'. The Trotters are about to enter the world of canine care, acting as paid dog sitters for Boycie and Marlene's puppy, as the affluent couple take a holiday in the Seychelles. As Del and Rodney discover when they pick the dog up, Duke is rather large for a puppy, understandable perhaps seeing as he is a Great Dane. After just one day living with the Trotters, Duke falls into a comatose state and is rushed to the vet. Salmonella poisoning is suspected as Duke has eaten warmed up pork leftovers for breakfast, the same batch of pork that Albert has just consumed along with pickles and crusty bread.

Starring: David Jason, Nicholas Lyndhurst, Buster Merryfield, John Challis, Sue Holderness.

Trotter Trivia: Although her name had been mentioned on a number of previous occasions, this was the first episode to feature the character of Marlene on screen.

Series 4 Episode 6
Watching the Girls Go By

Broadcast Date: 28 March 1985

Audience Figure: 14.4 million

Synopsis: Love is the topic of discussion at Nelson Mandela House. While Del's vision of love bears a strong resemblance to a yoghurt commercial, Uncle Albert reveals he still has strong feelings for a nine-fingered barmaid called Helga whom he met near the docks in Hamburg just after the war. Meanwhile Rodney is feeling rather lovelorn. He has rashly made a bet with Mickey Pearce that he is going to bring a girl along to the upcoming big party at The Nag's Head but has nobody to ask. When he hears how much money is at stake, Del decides to help his brother meet a girl and so takes Rodney to a number of local bars. Believing one of the bars to be a 'trouble place', Rodney does not hold out much hope of meeting a nice girl, so is pleasantly surprised when a young lady named Yvonne comes across and introduces herself. Luckily, she is free on the night of the party too...

Starring: David Jason, Nicholas Lyndhurst, Buster Merryfield, Roger Lloyd Pack, John Challis, Kenneth MacDonald, Patrick Murray, Nula Conwell, Carolyn Allen.

Series 4 Episode 7
As One Door Closes

Broadcast Date: 4 April 1985

Audience Figure: 14.2 million

Synopsis: Del is sure he is going to make a pretty profit on his latest venture, supplying louvre doors to old foe Brendan O'Shaughnessy, who has just landed a contract to decorate and fit out a new housing estate. The only snag is that the initial purchase of these doors from Teddy Cummins is going to require a £2000 investment, a sum which Trotters Independent Traders does not have. Del can see light at the end of the tunnel however when he finds out that Denzil has just been made redundant, meaning his old mate must have received a nice sum in redundancy money, a sum which is soon in Del's pocket. Having purchased the doors, disaster strikes when the architect in charge of the new estate changes his mind, leaving Del with a job lot of louvre doors and Denzil's five angry brothers on his trail. Could a rare and very valuable butterfly spotted in Greenwich Park be the answer to Del's prayers?

Starring: David Jason, Nicholas Lyndhurst, Buster Merryfield, Paul Barber.

Christmas Special

To Hull and Back

Broadcast Date: 25 December 1985

Audience Figure: 16.9 million

Synopsis: Boycie and Abdul have partnered up in business and are involved in a risky but potentially lucrative scheme to smuggle diamonds out of Amsterdam. Not wanting to take any personal risks, Boycie and Abdul recruit Del as a courier, promising him £15,000 if he carries out the job successfully. As old enemy Chief Inspector Slater is assigned to the diamond smuggling case, Del, Boycie and Abdul meet in secret in the back of Denzil's lorry. Unfortunately, Denzil sets off on his scheduled trip to Hull with Del still in the back. After a nightmare journey, Del is eventually rescued by Rodney but finds himself on the docks at Hull. As Slater has his men patrolling the airports, Del decides to fool the law by hiring a boat and sailing across to Amsterdam and back. All they need is an experienced sailor to take the helm. Step forward old sea dog Uncle Albert!

Starring: David Jason, Nicholas Lyndhurst, Buster Merryfield, John Challis, Roger Lloyd Pack, Jim Broadbent, Christopher Mitchell, Tony Anholt.

Trotter Trivia: The very first feature-length *Only Fools and Horses* episode and the first not to feature a laughter track.

Series 5 Episode 1

From Prussia with Love

Broadcast Date: 31 August 1986

Audience Figure: 12.1 million

Synopsis: It has been a busy night in The Nag's Head and Mike has just called time behind the bar. However, he is not sure how to communicate this to a German girl who has been sitting on her own for the entire evening and does not appear to speak English. After Albert fails to impress with his German language skills, Rodney steps forward to help the damsel in distress, only to find she is heavily pregnant. Ever the gentleman, Rodney invites Anna, who is on a student exchange scheme from Germany, to stay at the flat. Initially against the idea of having someone in the flat who could be "carrying a bellyful of people", Del starts to change his mind when Anna reveals she wants to put the baby up for adoption. With Boycie and Marlene longing for a child but unable to conceive, Del spots a golden opportunity.

Starring: David Jason, Nicholas Lyndhurst, Buster Merryfield, John Challis, Sue Holderness, Kenneth MacDonald, Erika Hoffman.

Trotter Trivia: This episode was initially planned to be part of series four and the original script featured Grandad but was rewritten to include Uncle Albert after Lennard Pearce's death.

Series 5 Episode 2

The Miracle of Peckham

Broadcast Date: 7 September 1986

Audience Figure: 14.2 million

Synopsis: The morning after a drunken night out, Rodney is horrified to discover he not only insulted the large and rather terrifying local trumpet player Biffo but also stole the big man's prized instrument. Del hasn't got time to worry about Rodney's problems as, much to the family's surprise, he is off to church. While Rodney and Albert wonder if Del is trying to work some sort of money-making scheme, the wheeler-dealer is witness to a holy miracle as the statue of Mary in the church begins to weep. Desperately needing funds in order to save the local hospice, Father O'Keefe reluctantly allows Del to spreads the word about the miracle to the world's media. It isn't long before Del Boy is being hailed as a modern prophet but is there a rather more simple explanation for his new found ability to predict when the miracle will next occur?

Starring: David Jason, Nicholas Lyndhurst, Buster Merryfield, P.G. Stephens, John Pierce Jones, Carol Cleveland.

Trotter Trivia: Most famous for her appearances with Monty Python, Carol Cleveland makes a cameo appearance at the end of the episode as an American TV news reporter.

Series 5 Episode 3

The Longest Night

Broadcast Date: 14 September 1986

Audience Figure: 16.7 million

Synopsis: After receiving less than friendly service from the checkout girl at Top Buy Superstore during their weekly grocery shop, the Trotters decide they will take their custom elsewhere in the future. As they leave the store, they are stopped by head of security Tom Clark and asked to accompany him to the manager's office. Spotting a promotional poster offering £1000 to the store's millionth customer, the Trotters believe they are about to receive a windfall. Instead, they find themselves accused of shoplifting and detained in the company of Clark and the store manager. The group are soon joined by another shoplifter, a small time criminal who calls himself The Shadow and who has designs on robbing the safe. Del recognises the young 'man of mystery' as Lennox Gilbey, the son of a proud church-going lady and tries to talk him out of going through with the crime. However, the night has a further twist in store.

Starring: David Jason, Nicholas Lyndhurst, Buster Merryfield, Vas Blackwood, John Bardon, Max Harvey.

Series 5 Episode 4
Tea for Three

Broadcast Date: 21 September 1986

Audience Figure: 16.5 million

Synopsis: Uncle Albert is feeling down as he has just heard news that his estranged wife Ada has been rushed to hospital. Del and Rodney's plan to cheer Albert up by taking him for a Chinese meal is put on hold when Trigger's niece Lisa pays her uncle a visit in The Nag's Head. The Trotter brothers are both smitten by the beautiful young woman and invite her to tea at Nelson Mandela House, their competitive spirit coming to the fore as both vie for her affections. Albert is concerned that history will repeat itself as he recounts how he and Grandad fought over Aunt Ada, leading to the brothers never speaking to each other again. Albert's concerns are ignored however, as Del leaves his brother asleep under a sun bed turned up to maximum, leading the literally red-faced Rodney to plot a revenge involving a trip to Hampshire, a make-believe car phone and a hang glider.

Starring: David Jason, Nicholas Lyndhurst, Buster Merryfield, Roger Lloyd Pack, Kenneth MacDonald, Gerry Cowper.

Trotter Trivia: The characters of Lisa and Andy returned for the 1987 Christmas special *The Frog's Legacy*.

Series 5 Episode 5

Video Nasty

Broadcast Date: 28 September 1986

Audience Figure: 17.5 million

Synopsis: The art class at the local evening school has been awarded a £10,000 grant to make a community film and Rodney is honoured to be asked to write the script. However, with Mickey Pearce due to direct and Rodney suffering from writer's block, suddenly the project doesn't seem such a good idea after all. Dismissing an enthusiastic Del's outline for a blockbuster action whodunit called *There's a Rhino Loose in the City,* Rodney continues to search for inspiration, while Del enlists a huge cast of extras from the community, for a nominal fee payable to himself of course. Meanwhile, Mickey finds himself with a video camera at his disposal, allowing him to do a bit of work for Boycie on the side, directing films of an adult nature. Using the Trotter flat as a location for their latest production, Mickey and his star Amanda are thrown out by Rodney before things go too far. Believing that to be the end of it, Rodney is horrified when Boycie holds a private screening in the back room of The Nag's Head for his latest production, *Night Nurse,* set in a rather familiar looking flat.

Starring: David Jason, Nicholas Lyndhurst, Buster Merryfield, Roger Lloyd Pack, John Challis, Sue Holderness, Kenneth MacDonald, Patrick Murray.

Series 5 Episode 6

Who Wants to be a Millionaire?

Broadcast Date: 5 October 1986

Audience Figure: 18.8 million

Synopsis: A familiar face from the past has returned to Peckham. Almost twenty years after emigrating to Australia, Del's former business partner Jumbo Mills is back in the country to work out a deal with Boycie concerning the import of luxury European cars. Never forgetting that Del gave him his last £200 to help him get to Australia all those years ago, Jumbo is also looking to repay his old friend for his generosity. He invites Del to be a partner in his luxury car business in Sydney, virtually guaranteeing Del that next year he will actually be the millionaire that he has always dreamed of being. With Rodney on board as 'executive' car cleaner, it looks like the Trotter family are Australia bound, minus Uncle Albert, who states that his travelling days are over. Promising to look after Albert financially, it seems that nothing can stop the Trotter boys finally realising their dream, until Rodney is denied a visa due to a previous minor drug offence. With the offer from Jumbo to come to Australia still open, will Del finally become that millionaire or are the bonds of brotherly love too strong to break?

Starring: David Jason, Nicholas Lyndhurst, Buster Merryfield, John Challis, Kenneth MacDonald, Nick Stringer.

Trotter Trivia: This was originally planned to be the final episode of *Only Fools and Horses* as David Jason had expressed a desire to move on to other projects. However, he changed his mind and the script was changed to incorporate a new ending.

Christmas Special

A Royal Flush

Broadcast Date: 25 December 1986

Audience Figure: 18.8 million

Synopsis: Tasked once more with being a lookout at the market for Del, Rodney's attention is drawn to a pretty young woman with an art stall. Plucking up the courage to speak to her, Rodney is impressed when he discovers the artwork on display is all the work of the young lady herself. Revealing her name to be Victoria, she agrees to have a bite to eat with Rodney in Sid's café. During their conversation, Victoria

129

reveals that she is the only daughter of the Duke of Maylebury and that her full title is Lady Victoria Marsham Hales. Needless to say this leaves Rodders more than a little gobsmacked. However, the unlikely pairing strike up a relationship and it isn't long before Rodney is invited to a clay pigeon shooting weekend at the Duke of Maylebury's estate. Spotting an opportunity to mix with high society and increase the Trotter bank balance along the way, Del unfortunately ensures Rodney's worst fears come true when he and Albert turn up unexpectedly at the shoot and wangle an invitation to dinner.

Starring: David Jason, Nicholas Lyndhurst, Buster Merryfield, Roger Lloyd Pack, Roy Heather, Sarah Duncan, Diane Langton, Jack Hedley

Trotter Trivia: Sarah Duncan, who played Lady Victoria in this episode, went on to become a successful novelist.

Christmas Special

The Frog's Legacy

Broadcast Date: 25 December 1987

Audience Figure: 14.5 million

Synopsis: Trigger's niece Lisa and her fiancé Andy, last seen helping Del into a hang glider in *Tea for Three,* are finally tying the knot and many of the regulars from The Nag's Head have been invited to the lavish wedding in Hampshire. While Boycie insists that he and Marlene circulate at the wedding reception, Del bumps into his mum's old friend Renee Turpin, who also happens to be Trigger's aunt. Nostalgically chatting about old times, Renee accidentally lets slip a tale of a buried stash of gold bullion which belonged to the late gentleman thief Freddy Robdal, a close friend of Del's mum Joan. With Freddie having left all his worldly goods to Joan and then she, in turn, bequeathing everything to Del and Rodney, it seems the Trotter boys are sitting on a fortune. The only snag is that nobody knows where the gold is buried. Could Rodney, in his new job as an undertaker's assistant, be the one to track down the late Freddie the Frog's treasure?

Starring: David Jason, Nicholas Lyndhurst, Buster Merryfield, Roger Lloyd Pack, John Challis, Sue Holderness, Kenneth MacDonald, Joan Sims, Gerry Cowper, Adam Hussein.

Trotter Trivia: This was the final episode to be produced by Ray Butt, who had been with the production from the start.

Christmas Special

Dates

Broadcast Date: 25 December 1988

Audience Figure: 16.6 million

Synopsis: Things couldn't be going better for Trotter's Independent Traders. Business is booming and the money is pouring in. While Del and Rodney celebrate, Uncle Albert is in a more reflective mood, nostalgically looking back at old photographs from his days in the navy and reminiscing about past birthdays. Could the crafty old sea dog be not so subtly trying to drop hints about his upcoming birthday? While Del speaks to Mike about holding a party for Albert in The Nag's Head, the whole pub is amazed when Trigger announces he has a date, arranged by a new dating agency in the high street. Never one to turn down the chance of female company, Del signs up with the agency and soon finds himself on a date with a young actress called Raquel. With love quickly blooming between the two, Del is disappointed when Raquel can't attend Albert's birthday due to her existing commitments as a drama teacher. Still, there is much fun to be had at the birthday bash, as Del has arranged for a stripogram to surprise Albert, a stripogram that looks very familiar...

Starring: David Jason, Nicholas Lyndhurst, Buster Merryfield, Roger Lloyd Pack, John Challis, Kenneth

MacDonald, Tessa Peake-Jones, Roy Heather, Andree Bernard.

Trotter Trivia: Dates features the very first appearance of Tessa Peake-Jones as Raquel and also Andree Bernard as Nervous Nerys.

Series 6 Episode 1

Yuppy Love

Broadcast Date: 8 January 1989

Audience Figure: 13.9 million

Synopsis: After watching the film *Wall Street* on multiple occasions, Del now is firmly of the opinion that image is everything. With his silver briefcase, Filofax and trench coat, Del has joined the Yuppie set and wants everyone to know that he is on his way to the top. None of this impresses Rodney however. The younger Trotter brother believes that the ruthless pursuit of wealth is immoral and is especially upset when Del reveals he is applying to buy the flat from the council so he can then immediately sell it for a nice profit. Objecting to Del's dream of moving into a large house in wealthy King's Avenue, Rodney's attention is soon swayed by a pretty and well-to-do young girl at evening school called Cassandra. Bumping into each other again later that same evening at a nightclub, Cassandra offers Rodney a lift home afterwards, the morally conflicted Trotter directing her to a house in King's Avenue.

Starring: David Jason, Nicholas Lyndhurst, Buster Merryfield, Roger Lloyd Pack, Gwyneth Strong, Patrick Murray, Steven Woodcock.

Trotter Trivia: Yuppy Love featured the debut of Gwyneth Strong as Cassandra.

Series 6 Episode 2

Danger UXD

Broadcast Date: 15 January 1989

Audience Figure: 16.1 million

Synopsis: While Del is having trouble with a job lot of video recorders purchased from Ronnie Nelson, Denzil is suffering from even worse luck. Planning to take out wife Corrine to celebrate their anniversary, Denzil first has to pick up fifty dolls which need to be returned to the factory that manufactured them. Running late, he decides to leave the dolls on the van until Monday so that he and Corrine can enjoy their night out. All is well until the factory burns down over the weekend, leaving Denzil stuck with a consignment of dolls. Immediately spotting an opportunity for some quick cash, Del takes the dolls off Denzil's hands. After all, it shouldn't be too difficult selling children's dolls down the market, should it? However, with the dolls being christened with names such as Lusty Linda and Erotic Estelle and turning out to be of the inflated variety, it looks like Del will need to adjust his target market slightly.

Starring: David Jason, Nicholas Lyndhurst, Buster Merryfield, Roger Lloyd Pack, John Challis, Gwyneth Strong, Paul Barber, Kenneth MacDonald.

Series 6 Episode 3

Chain Gang

Broadcast Date: 22 January 1989

Audience Figure: 16.3 million

Synopsis: Del has made a new acquaintance at the One-Eleven Club, a recently retired jeweller called Arnie. Although he had to give up working in the jewellery business due to heart problems, Arnie reveals to Del that he still likes to dabble occasionally and currently has a case of 250 24-carat

133

gold chains for sale at a bargain price. Unable to raise the required capital on his own, Del puts together a consortium consisting of himself, Boycie, Trigger, Mike, Albert and a reluctant Rodney. With the chains confirmed as genuine by an independent jeweller, the consortium's celebrations are short-lived as the original buyer, who pulled out of the deal, changes his mind and now wants the chains for himself. Revealed by Arnie to be a violent character, the consortium agree to sell the chains to Mr Stavros through Arnie, with the deal set to take place at a local restaurant. With all of the consortium on stakeout duties, nothing can go wrong. Unless Arnie does something stupid like have a heart attack in the middle of the restaurant...

Starring: David Jason, Nicholas Lyndhurst, Buster Merryfield, Roger Lloyd Pack, John Challis, Kenneth MacDonald, Gwyneth Strong, Paul Barber, Philip McGough.

Series 6 Episode 4

The Unlucky Winner Is

Broadcast Date: 29 January 1989

Audience Figure: 17 million

Synopsis: Rodney and Cassandra are taking advantage of having the flat to themselves by enjoying a quiet night flicking through Rodney's art portfolio, eating smoked salmon sandwiches and drinking wine. While Cassandra is quite taken with fourteen and a half year old Rodney's painting entitled *Marble Arch at Dawn*, Rodney is not so impressed with the fact that Del is using his portfolio to store all of his competition entries, as evidenced by a stray label from a tin of baked beans. Entering every competition he can lay his hands on, Del enters the fabled *Marble Arch at Dawn* into an art contest run by Mega Flakes, unbeknown to his younger brother of course. To Del's amazement, the painting wins first prize, an all-expenses paid holiday to Majorca. Rodney and Cassandra, accompanied by Del, are soon jetting off to the sun, their high spirits destined to be dampened when they learn that Rodney was actually victorious in the under fifteen year-old category.

Starring: David Jason, Nicholas Lyndhurst, Buster Merryfield, Gwyneth Strong, Kenneth MacDonald, Gina Bellman, Michael Fenton Stevens.

Trotter Trivia: The character of Elsie Partridge is mentioned for the first time in this episode before appearing on screen in the next, *Sickness and Wealth.*

Series 6 Episode 5
Sickness and Wealth

Broadcast Date: 5 February 1989

Audience Figure: 18.2 million

Synopsis: Despite suffering from severe stomach cramps, Del is determined to carry on as normal with no intention of going to see a doctor. With the bills piling up and wintry weather hampering sales of a consignment of summer dresses, Del has plenty of other things to worry about, let alone a dodgy tummy. With things looking bleak, the Trotter coffers are thrown a lifeline when Albert reveals his girlfriend Elsie Partridge is a retired medium, whose services were once sought after by people from miles around. Never one to let a money-making opportunity pass by, Del has soon whipped up a price list for Elsie's spiritual services, including rates for contacting departed friends, relatives, family pets and Elvis Presley. During a trial run séance above the Nag's Head, Del is surprised to receive a message from across the veil supposedly from his mum, urging him to see a doctor about his stomach pains. Will Del listen to his late mother and conquer his fear of doctors?

Starring: David Jason, Nicholas Lyndhurst, Buster Merryfield, Roger Lloyd Pack, John Challis, Sue Holderness,

Gwyneth Strong, Kenneth MacDonald, Andree Bernard, Constance Chapman.

Series 6 Episode 6

Little Problems

Broadcast Date: 12 February 1989

Audience Figure: 18.9 million

Synopsis: Although he should be happy that he and Cassandra are soon to be married, Rodney is worried. Not only does he have to find £2000 to put towards a deposit on a new flat, the younger Trotter is concerned he has failed his computer studies exam, meaning he won't be able to get a job working at his future father-in-law's printing firm. Always looking out for his little brother, Del promises to give Rodney the deposit money as a wedding present. Despite promising the money, Del hasn't actually got £2000 to spare, so needs to start calling in his debts. First port of call is Boycie, who owes him £3000 for a consignment of video recorders. Meanwhile, a job lot of mobile phones purchased on sale or return should also bring in a healthy sum, After Mickey and Jeavon reveal they originally purchased the phones from the Driscoll Brothers, who want their money immediately, Del has a tough decision to make; keep his promise to his brother or save himself from receiving a severe beating at the hands of South London's most feared gangsters.

Starring: David Jason, Nicholas Lyndhurst, Buster Merryfield, Roger Lloyd Pack, John Challis, Sue Holderness, Gwyneth Strong, Kenneth MacDonald, Paul Barber, Patrick Murray, Steven Woodcock, Denis Lill,

Trotter Trivia: Not long before filming for this episode began, Patrick Murray badly injured his arm after an accident involving a glass door. John Sullivan incorporated Patrick's heavily strapped arm into the script by having Mickey and Jeavon receive multiple injuries after a beating from the Driscoll Brothers.

Christmas Special

The Jolly Boys Outing

Broadcast Date: 25 December 1989

Audience Figure: 20.12 million

Synopsis: Rodney and Cassandra are celebrating their first wedding anniversary by throwing a dinner party. Looking to impress her work superiors at the bank, Cassandra invites her boss Steven and his wife Joanne. The only problem is, Del and Albert are coming too. After a discussion on banana sizes and an interesting game of Trivial Pursuit, Del reveals to a disapproving Cassandra that Rodney is going on the upcoming annual Jolly Boys Outing to Margate over the Bank Holiday weekend. With the coach freshly fitted with a new stereo courtesy of Del and a mountain of sandwiches made by Trigger, the boys are off to Margate. While the trip is delayed when Rodney is unexpectedly arrested, the day in Margate is enjoyed by all, despite Trigger losing his dolphin. The journey back to Peckham proves to be slightly more problematic when the coach spectacularly explodes before departure, due in no small part to the new stereo. With a rail strike causing further misery, the coach party is forced to find accommodation in Margate itself, already full to the brim with Bank Holiday revellers. Finding the atmosphere in the Villa Bella boarding house less than friendly, Del and Rodney take in the delights of the Mardi Gras cabaret club, where the resident magician's female assistant looks exceedingly familiar...

Starring: David Jason, Nicholas Lyndhurst, Buster Merryfield, Roger Lloyd Pack, John Challis, Sue Holderness, Gwyneth Strong, Tessa Peake-Jones, Kenneth MacDonald, Paul Barber, Patrick Murray, Roy Heather, Steven Woodcock, Denis Lill, Wanda Ventham.

Trotter Trivia: The Dreamland amusement park in Margate, where the funfair scenes were filmed for this episode, closed to the public in 2005. Happily, it reopened in 2015 after many years of campaigning and is still going strong as of the time of writing.

137

Christmas Special

Rodney Come Home

Broadcast Date: 25 December 1990

Audience Figure: 18 million

Synopsis: All is not well in the marriage between Rodney and Cassandra. While Cassandra is determined to forge ahead with her career at the bank, Rodney believes she is not paying enough attention to him. An almighty row ensues and Rodney ends up moving back into the flat at Nelson Mandela House, much to Del's chagrin, as Raquel is now living there too. On the advice of Mickey Pearce, Rodney concocts a plan to make Cassandra jealous by taking another woman out on a date, namely the receptionist from the Peckham Exhaust Centre. Desperately trying to stop his brother completely destroying his marriage, Del tries to fix the situation but only ends up making it worse when he tells Cassandra about Rodney's plan.

Starring: David Jason, Nicholas Lyndhurst, Buster Merryfield, Gwyneth Strong, Tessa Peake-Jones, Patrick Murray, Denis Lill, Tony Marshall.

Series 7 Episode 1

The Sky's the Limit

Broadcast Date: 30 December 1990

Audience Figure: 15 million

Synopsis: With his marriage on the rocks and his wife taking time out in Spain, Rodney is still living at Nelson Mandela House and has begun to drink heavily. After another heavy night in The Nag's Head, Rodney asks Albert to phone work to inform them he is not feeling well and therefore won't be in. Fearing that Rodney is putting his job at the printing firm at risk, Del meets with Cassandra's dad Alan to try and smooth things over.

Meanwhile Boycie is busy playing with his latest acquisition, a state of the art satellite dish that can pick up programmes from all over the world. After the dish is stolen, Boycie puts up a large reward for its return, a reward that Del is looking to grab after coming into possession of a similar dish from Boycie's brother-in-law Bronco. Did Bronco really steal Boycie's satellite or has he taken it from another location? Breaking news of the theft of a transmitter dish from the end of Gatwick's main runway puts a whole new light on the matter.

Starring: David Jason, Nicholas Lyndhurst, Buster Merryfield, Roger Lloyd Pack, John Challis, Sue Holderness, Gwyneth Strong, Tessa Peake-Jones, Kenneth MacDonald, Denis Lill,

Trotter Trivia: The TV newsreader in this episode was played by real-life news anchor Richard Whitmore, a familiar face on BBC news programmes for many years.

Series 7 Episode 2
Chance of a Lunchtime

Broadcast Date: 6 January 1991

Audience Figure: 16.6 million

Synopsis: Looking to revive her acting career, Raquel has landed an audition for the part of Rosalind in a stage production of Shakespeare's *As You Like It*. Revealing that he used to act at school, Del is a little too enthusiastic when helping Raquel learn her lines and then unexpectedly turns up at a lunch meeting that Raquel has with the director of the play. Later that evening, despite getting the part, Raquel is unhappy and Del is concerned that she is being distant with him. Fearing that Raquel may change once she begins to mix with the acting fraternity, Del is completely taken aback when Raquel reveals some other, very unexpected and happy news. Life in the Trotter flat will never be the same again.

Starring: David Jason, Nicholas Lyndhurst, Buster Merryfield, Roger Lloyd Pack, John Challis, Sue Holderness, Gwyneth Strong, Tessa Peake-Jones, Kenneth MacDonald, Denis Lill.

Series 7 Episode 3

Stage Fright

Broadcast Date: 13 January 1991

Audience Figure: 16.6 million

Synopsis: With Raquel three months pregnant and Rodney newly unemployed, Del feels the need for Trotters Independent Traders to once more diversify. The perfect opportunity presents itself when Eric, an old friend of Del, reveals he is having trouble booking a cabaret act for his club The Starlight Rooms. The newly formed Trotter International Star Agency is only too happy to help, in exchange for a £600 fee. Persuading Raquel to come out of retirement for one night, on the proviso that someone else performs alongside her, Del begins the hunt for a singing partner. Following Trigger's recommendation, Del books Tony Angelino, a flamboyant refuse collector dubbed The Singing Dustman. The only trouble is, Tony has a vocal 'problem' and can only sing certain songs, a warning that Del unfortunately ignores.

Starring: David Jason, Nicholas Lyndhurst, Buster Merryfield, Roger Lloyd Pack, John Challis, Gwyneth Strong, Tessa Peake-Jones, Kenneth MacDonald, Philip Pope.

Series 7 Episode 4

The Class of '62

Broadcast Date: 20 January 1991

Audience Figure: 16.2 million

Synopsis: Using the far from reliable fax machine sold to him by Del, Mike sends a message informing Del Boy that he has been invited to a school reunion that evening at The Nag's Head. While Raquel absorbs the news that her solicitors have managed to trace her estranged husband, Del and Rodney meet up with Trigger, Boycie and Denzil in the function room of The Nag's Head, anxiously wondering who the mystery organiser of the night's proceedings is. While Rodney likens the mystery to an Agatha Christie novel, Denzil worries that it could be their psychotic former headmaster Bend Over Benson. Trigger suspects Jeremy Beadle. With the room descending into panic, the lights go out and the door slowly opens to reveal a shadowy figure. As the light is switched back on, the mystery man is revealed to be none other than old enemy Roy Slater. Has the former disgraced detective really turned over a new leaf as he claims or is there another reason behind his return to Peckham?

Starring: David Jason, Nicholas Lyndhurst, Buster Merryfield, Roger Lloyd Pack, John Challis, Tessa Peake-Jones, Kenneth MacDonald, Paul Barber, Jim Broadbent.

Series 7 Episode 5

He Ain't Heavy, He's My Uncle

Broadcast Date: 27 January 1991

Audience Figure: 17.2 million

Synopsis: A recent spate of muggings in the local area has left Del concerned over the safety of his pregnant partner Raquel. Feeling it would be safer for Raquel to drive everywhere instead of walk, Del contacts Boycie to see what he can find in his price range. With a budget of just £400, Del buys a rusty Capri Ghia which Rodney quickly christens the Pratmobile. While Raquel is now reluctantly travelling around in the Capri Ghia, Uncle Albert believes his time spent boxing in the navy will help him ward off any potential muggers. Unfortunately, this belief is put to the test when, after a night in the Nag's Head spent chasing Marlene's mum Dora with old mate Knock-Knock, Albert is attacked on his way home. With Del and Rodney at odds over how to best handle the situation, Albert decides to leave home, fearing he has become a burden to his nephews.

Starring: David Jason, Nicholas Lyndhurst, Buster Merryfield, Roger Lloyd Pack, John Challis, Sue Holderness, Gwyneth Strong, Tessa Peake-Jones, Kenneth MacDonald.

Trotter Trivia: The soundtrack to this episode features the song *Uncle Albert/Admiral Halsey* by Paul and Linda McCartney, playing over the scenes of Del and Rodney searching the streets for their missing uncle.

Series 7 Episode 6

Three Men, a Woman and a Baby

Broadcast Date: 3 February 1991

Audience Figure: 18.9 million

Synopsis: With the flat on constant high alert due to the imminent arrival of Del and Raquel's baby, Rodney is more concerned over his continued marriage problems and the fact that 'he hasn't had a bit for months'. After a trip to Hampton Court simply leads to an argument with Cassandra over the best way to get out of the maze, Rodney thinks he may have more luck wooing his wife with a false ponytail, courtesy of Del's latest line of men's wigs. As Rodney and Cassandra finally make up at their flat, over at Nelson Mandela House Del is disappointed to see that one of the wigs is going bald. Resolving to call it the 'Bruce Willis Look', any worries Del has over the thinning hairpieces is soon forgotten as Raquel goes into labour.

Starring: David Jason, Nicholas Lyndhurst, Buster Merryfield, Roger Lloyd Pack, Gwyneth Strong, Tessa Peake-Jones, Kenneth MacDonald.

Trotter Trivia: Alongside *Little Problems, Three Men, a Woman and a Baby* attracted the highest audience figures of any regular *Only Fools & Horses* episode. This does not include any Christmas episodes or other specials.

Christmas Special
Miami Twice – The American Dream

Broadcast Date: 24 December 1991

Audience Figure: 17.7 million

Synopsis: The Trotter family and their friends are gathered together for the christening of Del and Raquel's son Damien. While Rodney is pleasantly surprised to receive a cheque from Alan for investments he made in a company pension scheme, Del is busy trying to make a deal with the vicar to supply regular shipments of 'pre-blessed' wine from Romania.Despite his windfall, Rodney is still unhappy. The slow pace at which he and Cassandra are rebuilding their marriage is frustrating him, while he is also jealous of Boycie and Marlene's impending holiday to the USA. In an effort to help his brother save his marriage, Del secretly cashes Rodney's cheque and books a week in Miami for two. Although Rodney is at first annoyed that Del has done this without asking, he soon comes round to the idea of he and Cassandra enjoying the Florida sunshine. His dreams come crashing down however as Cassandra reveals she can't travel on the dates booked due to a work seminar in Eastbourne. With the holiday booked in the name of Trotter, only someone with the same surname can take advantage of the spare ticket. Step up Del Boy!

Starring: David Jason, Nicholas Lyndhurst, Buster Merryfield, Roger Lloyd Pack, John Challis, Sue Holderness, Gwyneth Strong, Tessa Peake-Jones, Kenneth MacDonald, Paul Barber, Patrick Murray, Denis Lill, Wanda Ventham, Roy Heather.

Trotter Trivia: As Del and Rodney wait to board their Virgin flight to Miami, business mogul Richard Branson makes a cameo appearance as himself.

Christmas Special

Miami Twice – Oh, To Be In England

Broadcast Date: 25 December 1991

Audience Figure: 14.9 million

Synopsis: The Trotter boys have arrived in Miami but Rodney is dismayed to find that their accommodation for the week is a battered camper van that has definitely seen better days. Stopping off at an exclusive nightclub, the brothers are treated royally by the club owner who seems to recognise Del. This extra friendly treatment extends to a group of sharply dressed men who invite Del and Rodney to join them for the evening. Upon exiting the club, the Trotters discover that their camper van has been broken into and their luggage taken. Rico, the leader of the group who have just befriended them, invites Del and Rodney to come and stay with him at his palatial mansion. Although perturbed to see armed guards at the gate of the house, Del and Rodney can't believe their luck as they are put up in stunning bedrooms and given new clothes to wear. It seems that everywhere they go, Del is treated with utmost respect. Could this be because, as Del says, people just take to him wherever he goes or is the reason more to do with the fact that Rico is part of the local Mafia family, the head of which is the absolute spitting image of Del Boy?

Starring: David Jason, Nicholas Lyndhurst, Buster Merryfield, Roger Lloyd Pack, John Challis, Sue Holderness, Gwyneth Strong, Tessa Peake-Jones, Kenneth MacDonald, Paul Barber, Patrick Murray, Denis Lill, Roy Heather, Antoni Corone, Treva Etienne.

Trotter Trivia: Following on from Richard Branson in the previous episode, Bee Gee member Barry Gibb appears as himself here, tending to his garden as Del spots him from a boat cruise just offshore. "Alright, Bazza!"

Christmas Special
Mother Nature's Son

Broadcast Date: 25 December 1992

Audience Figure: 20.14 million

Synopsis: Del's application to buy the flat from the council has finally come through, leaving the Trotters facing an uncertain future as the mortgage figure is twice as much as the rent and Del couldn't even afford that. To add to Del's worries, now that he owns the flat, he is also responsible for clearing Grandad's old allotment which hasn't been touched for years. Looking to give his brother some hope and cheer, Rodney tells Del about his friend Miles, who has done exceedingly well for himself with a chain of natural food health stores. With healthy food and drink becoming fashionable, people are willing to pay high prices for goods such as natural spring water. This is golden news to Del Boy's ears, as there just so happens to be a rare urban water spring on Grandad's newly cleared allotment, one which only Del and Albert seem to be aware of.

Starring: David Jason, Nicholas Lyndhurst, Buster Merryfield, Roger Lloyd Pack, John Challis, Sue Holderness, Gwyneth Strong, Tessa Peake-Jones, Kenneth MacDonald, Paul Barber, Patrick Murray, Robert Glenister.

Trotter Trivia: The story of Del buying the flat from the council was first mentioned in the episode *Yuppy Love*, which opened series six back in 1989.

Christmas Special
Fatal Extraction

Broadcast Date: 25 December 1993

Audience Figure: 19.6 million

Synopsis: Christmas is fast approaching and Del is busy trying to make a deal with Ronnie Nelson over a consignment of Russian army camcorders which he believes will be a big seller over the festive period. As Ronnie is the owner of the One-Eleven Club, Del is spending much of his time in the casino, much to Raquel's chagrin. Fed up of Del's constant late nights out, Raquel decides to leave him and, along with Damien, moves in temporarily with Rodney and Cassandra. Feeling the pain not just from Raquel walking out on him but also from a troublesome tooth, Del impulsively asks Beverley, the receptionist from the dental surgery he visits, out on a date. After Rodney successfully talks him out of the date, Del calls Beverley to cancel and makes up with Raquel. Just as things seem to be looking up for Christmas, Del begins to spot Beverley wherever he seems to go, in the market, the pub and finally, to his horror, the flat...

Starring: David Jason, Nicholas Lyndhurst, Buster Merryfield, Roger Lloyd Pack, John Challis, Gwyneth Strong, Tessa Peake-Jones, Kenneth MacDonald, Paul Barber, Patrick Murray, Roy Heather, Mel Martin.

Trotter Trivia: After *Fatal Extraction* was screened, there would not be another new episode of *Only Fools and Horses* for three years.

Christmas Trilogy Part 1

Heroes and Villains

Broadcast Date: 25 December 1996

Audience Figure: 21.3 million

Synopsis: It has been three years since we last visited the Trotters and, as usual, things are not running smoothly. Rodney and Cassandra are trying desperately for a baby, while Del has just had an application for a home improvement grant from the council rejected. Meanwhile, Raquel is off to visit her estranged parents, after hearing from them for the first time in many years. With Cassandra deciding to spend some time at her parent's villa in Spain, the Trotter boys find themselves at a loose end for the weekend.

While Rodney is happy to stay at home, Del has his eye on the first prize in the local publicans' fancy dress ball being held on the Saturday night. After a reluctant Rodney is persuaded to go, his idea of dressing as the Blues Brothers is soundly rejected by Del in favour of some superhero themed outfits. When the van breaks down on their way to the ball, Del and Rodney - or rather, Batman and Robin – find themselves running through the back streets of Peckham to reach their destination.

Starring: David Jason, Nicholas Lyndhurst, Buster Merryfield, Roger Lloyd Pack, John Challis, Sue Holderness, Gwyneth Strong, Tessa Peake-Jones, Kenneth MacDonald, Paul Barber, Roy Heather, Angela Bruce.

Trotter Trivia: At the time of broadcast, *Heroes and Villains* attracted the highest ever audience figure for an *Only Fools and Horses* episode, until just four days later.

(Image copyright: British Broadcasting Corporation)

Christmas Trilogy Part 2

Modern Men

Broadcast Date: 27 December 1996

Audience Figure: 21.3 million

Synopsis: With Cassandra now expecting, Rodney feels he needs another job in order to be able to support his future family. Del is also looking to the future by taking inspiration from a book called *Modern Man*. Looking to be more considerate to Raquel, Del makes the sudden and rather surprising decision to have a vasectomy. Spotting a job advertised in the local paper that he thinks would suit him, Rodney rings the telephone number to apply. Believing he is speaking to a man called Ivor Hardy, Rodney soon realises he is talking to Del and is actually applying for his own job. Seemingly stuck with Trotter's Independent Traders for ever, Rodney soon has more pressing matters on his mind when news comes through that Cassandra has been rushed to hospital.

Starring: David Jason, Nicholas Lyndhurst, Buster Merryfield, Roger Lloyd Pack, John Challis, Sue Holderness, Gwyneth Strong, Tessa Peake-Jones, Kenneth MacDonald, Paul Barber, Patrick Murray, Roy Heather, Bhasker Patel.

Christmas Trilogy Part 3

Time on our Hands

Broadcast Date: 29 December 1996

Audience Figure: 24.3 million

Synopsis: Raquel is planning to throw a dinner party and is more nervous than usual because she has invited her parents to meet Del for the first time. Meanwhile, Del is worried about Rodney, as his younger brother is bottling up his emotions following Cassandra's miscarriage. After a dinner party unwittingly sabotaged by Albert accidentally mixing up the coffee and the gravy, Raquel's parents James and Audrey are invited to stay the night. The next morning, antique dealer James is stunned to find an incredibly rare timepiece in Del's garage, something which Del had always believed to be a Victorian egg-timer. Revealed to be the long-lost Harrison 'lesser watch', an almost mythical timepiece, the Trotters are advised to put the watch up for auction. Could Del and Rodney finally become the millionaires they have always dreamed of being?

Starring: David Jason, Nicholas Lyndhurst, Buster Merryfield, Roger Lloyd Pack, John Challis, Sue Holderness, Gwyneth Strong, Tessa Peake-Jones, Kenneth MacDonald, Paul Barber, Patrick Murray, Michael Jayston, Ann Lynn.

Trotter Trivia: The most watched *Only Fools and Horses* episode in history, *Time on our Hands* was also the last regular episode to feature Buster Merryfield.

Final Trilogy Part 1

If They Could See Us Now

Broadcast Date: 25 December 2001

Audience Figure: 21.35 million

Synopsis: Five years have passed since the Trotters achieved their dreams and became millionaires. However the dream has recently become a nightmare, with the crash of the Central American stock markets leading to the millionaire brothers losing all of their money. To add to the sorrow, news comes through that Uncle Albert has died. The old sea dog had been happily living in retirement on the south coast with his sweetheart Elsie Partridge. After a mix-up with the venue at Albert's funeral, Del and Rodney return to the flat at Nelson Mandela House, still owned by Derek, and try to work out a way of paying off their considerable debts. With things looking decidedly bleak, Del becomes a contestant on the hit TV game show *Gold Rush*, hosted by Jonathan Ross. With the whole of Peckham seemingly watching, can Del defy the odds and win the cash the Trotters so desperately need?

Starring: David Jason, Nicholas Lyndhurst, Roger Lloyd Pack, John Challis, Sue Holderness, Gwyneth Strong, Tessa Peake-Jones, Paul Barber, Patrick Murray, Roy Heather, Ben Smith.

Trotter Trivia: This episode was dedicated to Buster Merryfield and Kenneth MacDonald, who had both sadly died since the making of the 1996 Christmas trilogy.

Final Trilogy Part 2

Strangers on the Shore

Broadcast Date: 25 December 2002

Audience Figure: 17.4 million

Synopsis: As Mike is currently serving time in prison for embezzling the brewery, Sid is now in charge at The Nag's Head. Looking to cut a deal with Sid to supply him with cheap booze, Del spies a perfect opportunity to stock up on supplies when he and Rodney agree to attend a naval reunion in France on behalf of Uncle Albert. Not wishing to inform Rodney of his plan, Del secretly asks Denzil and Trigger to meet them with an empty truck at the wine warehouse in France. After representing Albert at the reunion, in a village where many of the male residents looks suspiciously like the promiscuous old sea dog, the Trotter brothers bump into Trigger and Denzil at the warehouse and Del's plan is revealed. While unloading the truck back at Nelson Mandela House, everyone is shocked to find another occupant in the back, an illegal immigrant who can't speak English but whose name appears to be Gary.

Starring: David Jason, Nicholas Lyndhurst, Roger Lloyd Pack, John Challis, Sue Holderness, Gwyneth Strong, Tessa

Peake-Jones, Paul Barber, Patrick Murray, Roy Heather, Ben Smith, James Ellis, Nabil Elouahabi.

Final Trilogy Part 3

Sleepless in Peckham

Broadcast Date: 25 December 2003

Audience Figure: 16.37 million

Synopsis: Life for the Trotter family is a mix of happiness and despair. On the happier side of things, Cassandra and Rodney are expecting once more but the downside to this joyful news is that everyone is still crammed into the flat at Nelson Mandela House. Still, this won't last much longer as the Trotters are due to be evicted from the flat soon anyway! Del and Rodney have not been able to raise the capital required to pay what they owe to the Inland Revenue so are on the verge of losing everything. Rodney tries to cheer Del up by enlarging a photograph owned by Sid of the 1960 Jolly Boys' Outing. The group shot features a young Del, Trigger, Boycie, Denzil and Sid, along with Grandad and, to his and Cassandra's shock, someone who looks alarmingly like Rodney himself.

Starring: David Jason, Nicholas Lyndhurst, Roger Lloyd Pack, John Challis, Sue Holderness, Gwyneth Strong, Tessa Peake-Jones, Paul Barber, Patrick Murray, Roy Heather.

(Image copyright: British Broadcasting Corporation)

Printed in Great Britain
by Amazon

51329778R00097